MIPLC Studies

Edited by

Prof. Dr. Christoph Ann, LL.M. (Duke Univ.)
TUM School of Management

Prof. Robert Brauneis
The George Washington University Law School

Prof. Dr. Josef Drexl, LL.M. (Berkeley)
Max Planck Institute for Innovation and Competition

Prof. Dr. Michael Kort
University of Augsburg

Prof. Dr. Thomas M.J. Möllers
University of Augsburg

Prof. Dr. Dres. h.c. Joseph Straus
Max Planck Institute for Innovation and Competition

Volume 31

Wael Zohni

Examining the Role of Patent Quality in Large-Scale "Patent War" Litigation

A Historical Comparison and Proposal for a Restorative U.S. Patent System

Nomos

MIPLC Munich Intellectual Property Law Center — Augsburg, München, Washington DC

The Deutsche Nationalbibliothek lists this publication in the
Deutsche Nationalbibliografie; detailed bibliographic data
are available on the Internet at http://dnb.d-nb.de

a.t.: Munich, Master Thesis Munich Intellectual Property Law Center, 2017

ISBN   978-3-8487-5107-5 (Print)
         978-3-8452-9309-7 (ePDF)

British Library Cataloguing-in-Publication Data
A catalogue record for this book is available from the British Library.

ISBN   978-3-8487-5107-5 (Print)
         978-3-8452-9309-7 (ePDF)

Library of Congress Cataloging-in-Publication Data
Zohni, Wael
Examining the Role of Patent Quality in Large-Scale "Patent War" Litigation
A Historical Comparison and Proposal for a Restorative U.S. Patent System
Wael Zohni
78 p.
Includes bibliographic references.

ISBN   978-3-8487-5107-5 (Print)
         978-3-8452-9309-7 (ePDF)

1st Edition 2018
© Nomos Verlagsgesellschaft, Baden-Baden, Germany 2018. Printed and bound in Germany.

Table of Contents

Charts and Figures

Abstract

The dramatic world-wide impact of the 'iPhone' smartphone has made Apple Corporation a topic of modern-day legend. Samsung's alleged "theft" of Apple's iPhone concept in March of 2010 led to the start of what has come to be known as the "Smartphone Wars," a cascade of litigation that has become just as legendary. Over one-hundred years prior, another well-known "patent war" concerning the establishment of modern aviation took place between the Wright Brothers and Glenn Curtiss. In this case, the Wrights viewed Glenn Curtiss as having stolen critical aspects of their claimed aircraft design enabling controlled flight. The Wrights pursued extensive litigation against Curtiss and others accordingly. Although widely separated by time and circumstance, these cases support similar negatively held notions of the patent system; namely, that it diverts valuable resources away from innovation and towards legal and business maneuvering. Anti-patent commentators refer to patent wars as evidence of burdensome transactional costs to society. On the other hand, proponents point out that such examples are an exception and that the patent system has facilitated benefits that far outweigh such costs. Reality appears to rest somewhere between these opposing views.

Although the U.S. Patent System has been essential to spurring innovation it has wavered in its efficiency and effectiveness at doing so. This paper first makes historical comparison and analysis of the *Apple* and *Wright* landmark patent war cases to illustrate that, irrespective of timing, benefits of a patent system fundamentally hinge on how well it defines and maintains "patent quality." Much of the challenge in maintaining such quality relates to the subjective and often uncertain nature of invention criteria such as "non-obviousness." As shown by recent trends, decreased patent quality leads to greater uncertainty about patent validity, which in turn invites more litigation.

This work then proposes that to improve constancy on patent quality the U.S. patent office should consider returning to original strategies envisioned by the Founders of the United States. This approach is outlined in Congressional House Resolution (H.R.) 10 passed in 1789. H.R. 10 describes a patent-registration system that emphasizes the utility of invention and reliance on public review to govern much of the patent granting process. After more than forty years, the U.S. patent office turned to an examination-based system, not because of flawed virtues with registration, but lack of supporting technical and logistical capabilities required for its proper execution. Modern technology can now be applied to achieve the original vision sketched out in H.R.10 to restore patent quality control systems. A "high-tech" patent registration system can obtain the self-governing aspects intended by the Founders by integrating a utility parameter and information technology into the application process.

Further discussion is provided to illustrate how a restorative U.S. patent registration system can utilize existing infrastructure in an undisruptive yet dramatically improved manner; helping avert future patent wars and other costly litigation. Finally, this paper revisits the *Apple* and *Wright* cases from a theoretical standpoint that considers proposed reforms.

Acronyms and Abbreviations

3G	3rd Generation of mobile phone standards
AIA	America Invents Act of 2012
API	Application Program Interface
Art.	Article
CEO	Chief Executive Officer
CHFP	Certified Human Factors Engineering Professional
EP	European Patent
EPO	European Patent Office
Fed. Cir.	Federal Circuit
GAO	Government Accounting Office
GPU	Graphical User Interface
H.R.	House Resolution
IP	Intellectual Property
ITC	International Trade Commission
JMOL	Judgment as a Matter of Law
LTD	Limited
MP3	MPEG-2 Audio Layer III
R&D	Research and Development
S. Ct.	Supreme Court
TUX	Total User Experience
USC	United States Code
USPTO	United States Patent and Trademark Office

I. Introduction

For many Americans the term "patent" is linked to a sense of tradition and cultural icons such as Thomas Edison, inventor of the operational incandescent light bulb. The very image of the light bulb itself has become a symbol for invention or a good idea.[1] Another commonly held notion is that a patent guarantees an individual protection from having his or her idea stolen by unscrupulous competitors. Such protection is to help ensure that the time and expense applied towards developing new products is not lost by those willing to invest such substantial efforts.[2] In fact, these views do represent the mission of the U.S. patent system. However, as one digs further into patent system practices and its history, it becomes apparent that these beliefs only reflect an often elusive ideal. How close the U.S. patent system actually comes to representing this ideal has varied over the years.[3]

Before considering the functionality of the patent system, there is the question of its necessity in the first place. Whether a patent system truly fosters benefits to individuals and society continues to be a topic of debate from both a historical and forward-looking perspective. Opponents of the patent system have long argued that granting inventors exclusive rights runs counter to anti-competitive foundations of a free-market economy by enabling profit interest to overtake the drive for legitimate innovation.[4] They also express that the task of identifying deserving ideas is itself problematic because all inventions leverage the work of predecessors to

---

1 Hunter Oatman-Stanford, *Let There Be Light Bulbs: How Incandescents Became the Icons of Innovation,* Collector's Weekly (July 2015) https://www.collectorswee kly.com/articles/let-there-be-light-bulbs/ (accessed Sep 1, 2017)
2 Drew Hendricks, *7 Simple Ways You Can Protect Your Idea From Theft,* Forbes (Nov. 2013), https://www.forbes.com/sites/drewhendricks/2013/11/18/7-simple-wa ys-you-can-protect-your-idea-from-theft/#7af8b02b1f86 (accessed Sep 2, 2017)
3 Richard A. Posner, *Why There Are Too Many Patents in America,* The Atlantic (July 2012), https://www.theatlantic.com/business/archive/2012/07/why-there-are-too-many-patents-in-america/259725/ (accessed Aug 30, 2017)
4 *An Economic Review of thePatent System: Hearing Before the Subcomm. on Patents, Trademarks, and Copyrights,* 85 Cong.33 39 (1958) (Report of Fritz Machlup)

some extent. Chemist and economist Michael Polanyi describes that any patent system "is essentially deficient, because it aims at a purpose which cannot be rationally achieved. It tries to parcel up a stream of creative thought into a series of distinct claims, each of which is to constitute the basis of a separately owned monopoly."[5]

On the other hand, proponents of the patent system describe a moral and common-sense need to sufficiently compensate those who invest the substantial time and resources required for accomplishing important innovation. Without an incentive very few would be willing to risk such resources. In this view, a patent provides compelling motivation in the form of securing fixed-term exclusive use rights to a new technology and corresponding market advantage to the inventor. Modern economic theory has generally accepted the "monopoly-profit-incentive" scheme to work.[6] Austrian theorist Friedrich von Wieser summarizes this common view with: "the patent right is granted to the inventor, in order to bring his technical leadership, his talents, and genius into the service of society."[7] Another well-known economist, A.T. Hadley, once stated that "a patent system, if properly guarded, seems to be thoroughly justified by its results. In the absence of such protection, few new inventions would be developed."[8]

There are legitimate concerns brought up by both sides of this debate. Overall it appears that the patent systems implemented in the US, Britain and elsewhere have been instrumental in driving individuals and companies to innovate new and useful technology and products. At the same time, even advocates of these systems acknowledge that maintaining an optimal patent system has been a challenging pursuit. Much of this challenge is due to the subjective nature of defining invention alluded to by Polanyi and others.

This uncertainty is said to lead to excessive conflict in the market that exacts a high toll from society by diverting resources from innovation to complex legal engagements. Some of the worst examples of such penalty

---

5 *Id.* at 29
6 *Id.* at 23
7 *Id.* at 33
8 *Id.* at 37

are "patent wars," prolonged and far-reaching litigation that usually surrounds a monumental technology market opportunity.[9]

The position of this paper is that moral considerations, "money-profit-incentive" and aims for societal benefit provide sound basis for establishment of the U.S. patent system. The dramatic rate of innovation witnessed in the 20th century and beyond suggests that the patent system has provided benefit; but whether it can continue to do so depends on, as A.T. Hadley puts it, whether it remains *"properly guarded."* This work argues that a central element to guarding a patent system is establishment of effective and reliable guidelines for determining what constitutes a "quality" patent.

As will be discussed, insufficiencies in both defining and enforcing a consistent standard for patent quality have been largely responsible for the heavy transactional costs described by opponents of the patent system.[10] The value and perception of a U.S. patent have been diluted from that of a given right to that of "a chance of an exclusive right" as some modern economists have referred to it.[11] As will also be argued, this issue relates to the element of an invention's *utility* when considering perspectives that were present during early legislation of the U.S. patent system.

This paper will begin by examining the origins of the U.S. patent system before comparing two historic patent wars; that of *Apple v Samsung* (2012) concerning today's smartphone and *Wright v Herring-Curtiss* (1908) concerning invention of the modern airplane in 1903. Finally, analysis and concepts for further investigation will be proposed on the topic of enabling the U.S. patent system to effectively meet future challenges. Part of this enablement uses technology itself to achieve original constructs intended by Founders of the nation almost two-hundred and fifty years ago.

---

9 Kurt Eichenwald, *The Great Smartphone War*, Vanity Fair (May 2014), https://www.vanityfair.com/news/business/2014/06/apple-samsung-smartphone-patent-war (accessed Aug 29, 2017)

10 *Intellectual Property: Patent Office Should Define Quality, Reassess Incentives, and Improve Clarity*, Government Accountability Office, GAO-16-490, Report to Chairman, Committee on Judiciary, House of Representatives 1 (June 2016)

11 Described by Professor Joseph Drexl in lecture, IP and Competition Law (seminar), Munich Intellectual Property Law Center (June 2017)

A. The Patent Wars

The 20ᵗʰ century has ushered in a period of momentous progress in information technology including dramatic advances in mobile communication and computing devices. The worldwide smartphone sensation was started by Apple Corporation in 2007 with the introduction of their "iPhone 3." By combining smooth touchscreen functionality with stylish, compact design, Apple introduced a major disruption to the mobile phone market. Apple's rival, Samsung Corporation, acting somewhat as Google's proxy, responded by designing and manufacturing their line of "Galaxy" smartphones which took liberties with protected iPhone product features. Apple responded with a major litigation campaign with their famous founder, Steve Jobs, declaring "thermonuclear war" on Samsung. Jobs considered Samsung to have stolen the iPhone product concept and became dedicated to pursuing patent infringement lawsuits and injunctions accordingly.[12]

Another famed patent war occurring over one-hundred years prior, *Wright vs. Curtiss*, appears to have some interesting parallels to the modern *Apple vs. Samsung* case. In *Wright*, the world-changing invention was that of the airplane. In place of Steve Jobs there was Orville and Wilbur Wright, recognized pioneers of fixed-wing aircraft design. Corresponding to Samsung was Glenn Curtiss, a rival engineer who launched his aircraft business using elements contained in patents filed by the Wrights. Like Jobs' view of Samsung, Wilbur Wright considered Curtiss' actions open theft and dedicated himself to stopping his opponent at any cost. The Wright Company launched an extensive litigation campaign to prevent Curtiss as well as others from using what they viewed as their concept for controlled flight.[13]

Despite the dramatic similarities in these two patent wars, there are of course also substantial differences. *Apple* takes place in the modern information age against a sophisticated backdrop of intensified patent activity and fierce global corporate competition. *Wright* occurred in a compara-

---

12 Shara Tibken, *Apple v. Samsung patent trial recap: How it all turned out*, CNET (2014), https://www.cnet.com/news/apple-v-samsung-patent-trial-recap-how-it-all -turned-out-faq/ (accessed Aug 30, 2017)

13 Matt Levy, *Yes, The Aviation Industry Was Nearly Derailed by the Wright Brothers' Patent*, Patent Progress (Jan 2015) https://www.patentprogress.org/2015/01/1 2/yes-aviation-industry-nearly-derailed-wright-brothers-patent/ (accessed Aug 25, 2017)

tively simple setting with a patent system that emphasized utility and economic advancement. Although both cases are considered patent wars the former could indeed be viewed as a "nuclear" war in comparison to the relatively conventional conflict of the latter. Modern patent wars have become dramatically larger in terms of number of patents and international implications. Establishment of voluminous patent portfolios as a form of deterrence and protection has today become a matter of policy with large firms such as Apple and Samsung. In both *Wright* and *Apple* however, observers and historians have argued that the time, resources and expense consumed by such large-scale litigation ultimately do not serve founding principles and objectives of the U.S. Patent System.[14]

B. *Purpose of Comparison*

Comparing the *Apple* and *Wright* patent wars helps to separate long-standing issues from temporary circumstantial situations that have faced the U.S Patent System. In the early 1900s for instance, patent office examination priorities emphasized proven demonstration of any flying machine-related claims; a stringent requirement that led to the rejection of initial patent filing attempts by the Wright brothers.[15] Modern day patent examination has reached the opposite extreme where relaxed criteria are allowing excessive patent grants.[16]

There are always challenges with properly "tuning" patent examination criteria to particular times and circumstances. Comparison of the *Apple* and *Wright* cases provides illustrative examples of this tuning process. Furthermore, plotting these two data points relative to the baseline defined by origins of the U.S. patent system can improve understanding of its fundamental issues. This paper intends to explore these historical representa-

---

14 Joe Nocera, *Greed and the Wright Brothers,* NY Times (Aug 2014), https://www.n ytimes.com/2014/04/19/opinion/nocera-greed-and-the-wright-brothers.html?_r=2 (accessed Aug 25, 2017)

15 Rodney K. Worrel, *The Wrights Brothers' Pioneer Patent*, 65 American Bar Association Journal 1513, 1514 (1979)

16 Lisa Rein, *Patent Lawsuits Swell and Watchdog Says the Government is to Blame,* Washington Post, (July 2016), https://www.washingtonpost.com/news/powerpost/ wp/2016/07/20/patent-office-tktk/?utm_term=.be6d9769eecb (accessed Aug 25, 2017)

tions before providing observations along with recommended approaches for future investigation.

II. Origins of the U.S. Patent System

A. Overview

Article I, Section 8, Clause 8, of the United States Constitution grants Congress the power "To promote the progress of science and useful arts, by securing for limited times to authors and inventors the exclusive right to their respective writings and discoveries."[17] Because this clause describes Congress' authority to pass legislation on copyrights and patents, it has become known as the "patent and copyright clause."[18] Although many details of early U.S. patent system history remain murky, it is apparent that the majority of Framers of the Constitution recognized a need for establishing a national patent system. This awareness was based on appreciation of historical patent customs and specifically the example set by the British system as a working model.[19] British patent custom at the time represented an exception to their Statute of Monopolies of 1623. Whereas the Statute specified a general ban on monopolies, it made a special exemption for rewarding inventions.[20]

Although the Framers relied heavily on English precedent, they also pursued a mechanism that was uniquely American to address the needs of a growing nation. A series of bills and acts from years 1789 through 1836 reflect these early attempts. Examining this first period helps identify original intentions by the Framers and establish a context for considering subsequent events concerning U.S. patent law.[21]

---

17 U.S. Const. art. I, § 8, cl. 8.

18 Cornell Law School, https://www.law.cornell.edu/wex/intellectual_property_claus e (accessed Sep 1, 2017)

19 Thomas T. Gordon et al., Patent Fundamentals for Scientists and Engineers, 7 (3d ed. 1995), https://books.google.de (accessed Aug 27, 2017)

20 Edward C. Walterscheid, To Promote the Progress of Useful Arts: American Patent Law and Administration, 1798-1836 11 (1998)

21 *Id.*

B. Pre-Constitutional Setting

As part of examining the origins of the patent clause, it is fitting to consider the historical setting in which the U.S. Constitution was drafted. Leading up to the American Revolutionary War, Britain's Parliament had pursued a policy of increased taxation on the American colonies through legislation such as the Sugar Act, Quartering Act of 1764 and Stamp Act of 1765.[22] Colonists thought it was unfair to have important policy decisions so far out of reach of America itself. This chief complaint of "no taxation without representation" became the American Revolutionary War cry.[23] Colonial leaders reacted against the British by establishing their own separate Continental Congress.

By March 1781, a preliminary constitution entitled the "Articles of Confederation" was ratified by this new Continental Congress. These Articles provided a minimal framework for a functioning central government with most authority remaining with individual states. This minimalist approach reflected the general suspicion American states held towards centralized power based on their experience with the British. [24]

The topic of patents was a low priority given all the other challenges of unifying the colonies at the time. It is therefore not surprising that no specified measure of promotion of the useful arts was included in this first document. However, it soon became clear that the new administration would need more power to function properly.[25]

The interval between the Articles of Confederation and ratification of the U.S. Constitution reflects a challenging and foundational phase for the development of the United States. The Founders struggled with balancing needs for sufficient centralized power against lingering concerns with such authority. Still, intellectual property stood out as being important enough to be included in the final document. The British patent system, with its

---

22 William S. Price, Jr., *Reasons Behind the Revolutionary War*, Tar Heel Junior Historian Association, NC Museum of History (1992) taken from NCMedia, http://www.ncpedia.org/history/usrevolution/reasons (accessed Aug 29, 2017)

23 *Id.*

24 History.com staff, *The Continental Congress*, (2010) History.com, http://www.history.com/topics/american-revolution/the-continental-congress (accessed Sep 5, 2017)

25 Walterscheid, *supra,* at 26

inexpensive reward system based on the grant of exclusive rights, had demonstrated this importance.[26]

A Constitutional Convention took place in Philadelphia, Pennsylvania during the summer of 1797. The goal was to modify the Articles into a more practicable document. Charles Pinckney, a delegate from South Carolina, brought his "South Carolina Plan." Although details remain unclear, it appears that Pinckney's Plan contained a proposal to grant Congress authority "to secure to authors the exclusive rights to their performances and discoveries." However, some deny his plan included these choice words.[27] None of the other state plans suggested language on an intellectual property clause; therefore details on how it was finalized within the U.S. Constitution remain obscure. The Articles of Confederation were replaced by the finalized U.S. Constitution in May 1789.[28]

The new federal government went into effect March 4, 1789, with Congress entering its first session through Sep 29, 1789. Some individuals presented patent applications as well as bills to promote the useful arts but were ignored due to other priorities during this phase. A second session ran from Jan 4, 1790 to Aug 12, 1790, at which time Congress took first steps to enact a system for securing exclusive rights to inventors for their discoveries and inventions. This first activity forms the basis of the U.S. patent system.[29]

C. House Resolution 10 (H.R. 10)

During its first sessions Congress was approached with several requests for exclusive rights by inventors based on the patent clause.[30] Amongst some of these early inventors was John Churchman who claimed methods for navigation using a needle compass and John Fitch for applying steam power to ships. Several fundamental questions regarding rights and procedures for handling patent prosecution and third party disputes naturally came up as a matter of course in these first few months.[31] These questions

---

26　*Id.* at 27
27　*Id.* at 35
28　History.com, *supra*
29　Walterscheid, *supra,* at 8
30　*Id.* at 81
31　*Id.* at 84-85

were difficult to resolve as there was only the patent clause contained in the Constitution to work with at that point. Therefore, Congress appointed a committee tasked with investigating these questions and determining "a bill to promote the progress of science and the useful arts."[32] The committee presented this first bill, designated *H.R.10* on June 23, 1789. H.R.10 was to become the precursor to the Patent Act of 1793.[33]

H.R.10 contains eights sections with the first two addressing copyright and the remaining six directed to patents.[34] Although it mostly followed the British model it introduced substantial departures such as adding more specific methodologies for implementing patent rights and not allowing patents of import. Section 3 presents patent application procedures that instruct inventors to "direct an advertisement to be inserted, at the costs and charges of the petitioner in some two of the public papers ___ for the term of ___ weeks, one at least in each week, giving notice of such application, and...requiring all persons concerned to appear before..at certain day and place..to shew cause why letters patent under the great seal of the United States, should not issue.." [35] This section describes a system wherein the concerned public would review applications in an expedited fashion to determine objections to any grant. This approach is "clearly intended to create a registration rather than an examination system, and in addition one that is modeled rather closely after the English system. Thus it provides for an American version of a caveat notice."[36]

The English caveat notice was a formal request made by a rights holder to the managing patent office to receive alerts of any third-party applications in a given subject matter. This signal provided the requestor an opportunity to contest any applications before they issued as patents. Because the English system did not include formal examination, the caveat system was the only way to interrogate new applications.[37] Section 3 appears to pursue similar ends but instead uses mass publications to provide more impartial exposure of the idea to the public as a whole. Section 4 of

---

32 *Id.* at 87
33 *Id.* at 98
34 *Id.* at 91
35 *Id.* at 92, 95
36 *Id.* at 98
37 28 Sean Bottomley, The British System during the Industrial Revolution 1700-1852, Cambridge IP and Information Law 53 (2014)

the bill calls for a proper description of the invention as was the English practice.[38]

Section 5 of H.R.10 provides a summary of procedures for handling challenges arising from section 4. It includes that "upon the notice,..any other person .. shall shew cause to..why letters patent..should not issue to the party petitioning ..shall refer the petition..to the chief justice, and one other justice of the supreme court.." It mostly follows the English model except it moves decision authority from the executive to the judiciary. In this way, it appears that H.R.10 was attempting to shorten the feedback loop that takes place between conflict and development of case law that updates guidelines for future engagements. The remaining sections of the bill deal with formalities such as filing procedures and fees.[39]

D. Patent Acts of 1790 and 1793

Following H.R.10 there was a flurry of activity that included several other House Resolutions before settlement on the first formal Patent Act of 1790. By that point, the registration system described by H.R.10 had temporarily given way to a formalized review process that assessed incoming patent applications. This examination would determine if the invention was "sufficiently useful and important." It is submitted that this methodology, unprecedented at the time, reveals a fundamental concern over *utility* that was to be considered alongside novelty as a means for avoiding frivolous or weak patents.[40]

This first attempt at examination lasted barely three years before having to make way for realities of an overwhelming flow of patent petitions. Amongst several other changes, the Patent Act of 1793 returned to the registration system described originally in H.R.10 due, in large part, to unrealistic expectations for completing a proper examination of all incoming applications. As historian Edward C. Walterscheid describes:

> "an examination system had been briefly tried and found wanting .. because the task of examination was found to be too burdensome..a registration system akin to that being used in Great Britain..appeared to be functioning rather well..and had the distinctly laudatory and desirable advantage of minimizing

---

38 Walterscheid, *supra,* at 99
39 *Id.* at 101
40 *Id.* at 14

the role of government and hence of governmental expense in implementing a system of patents."[41]

Although the Patent Act of 1793 did away with examination, the language of the legislation continued to emphasize utility and novelty. Section 1 maintained that inventions should represent "new and useful art, machine, manufacture, or composition of matter, or any ..improvement" similar to language that was in H.R.10. Section 2 makes distinctions between "discovery" and "improvement" patents; the former representing major ideas with broad application and the latter representing significant but comparatively incremental modifications inside the "shadow" of a major invention.[42]

E. The "Registration Years:" 1793 through 1836

With the Patent Act of 1793 U.S. patent law entered a more than forty-year "era of registration." As case law and public perception developed during this period so did criticisms of the patent system. The chief complaint from the public at large centered upon "fraudulent or worthless patents issued under the Act of 1793."[43] Despite the ideal framework described in the Act, there emerged problems with unscrupulous opportunists who took advantage of registration to attempt patents on trivial content. At that time patent letters contained the Seal of the President of the United States and therefore appeared intimidating to the uninitiated subjects of "enforcement" of such patents.[44] Complaints "that speculators were using 'frivolous' patents to prey on the public would be raised again and again. Thus..in 1830 William Elliot, chief clerk .. reiterated the need for authority 'for *refusing* patents ... to mere speculators (not inventors) who make a business in levying contributions on the public by licensees under the title of 'patents' for neither new nor useful inventions, .. and who fill the country with litigation."[45] As will be later detailed, limited access to relevant publications and information on patents by the general public eventually resulted in rejection of the patent registration system.

---

41 *Id.* at 15
42 *Id.* at 480
43 *Id.* at 18
44 *Id.* at 323
45 *Id.* at 325

This backlash led to the Patent Act of 1836, which set the basis of the examination-based U.S. patent system held to this day.

F. Summary

As a newly forming nation, the United States recognized the importance of intellectual property rights enough to include the special provision known as the "copyright and patent clause" in the Constitution. Although early legislation was based on the successful British patent custom, American law was more ambitious in codifying patent laws while simultaneously limiting the extent of government reach for granting "monopoly rights." Initial bills such as H.R.10 reflected these intentions by setting firm standards for usefulness and calling upon the public to assist in interrogating applications for patent registration.

Subsequent efforts at developing patent law have had to struggle with many issues including resources and unscrupulous speculators. Although an examination-based system was introduced in 1836, the framework defining the preceding "era of registration" still holds valuable indications on patent system implementation.

III. U.S. Patent Quality Today

A. Introduction

Fast-forwarding to the early 21st century it is remarkable that many of the issues the Framers dealt with are still being grappled with today. In 1790 there were only two or three individuals performing all patent examination whereas now the U.S. Patent and Trademark Office (USPTO) employs thousands of examiners.[46] Yet the patent office is still so overwhelmed with processing applications that turn-times are on the order of years and even then, patent grants are often questionable. A recent exposure on this state of affairs is found in a government assessment report from 2016.

B. Congressional Review of USPTO Performance

Dramatic increases in patent litigation have recently prompted U.S. Congress to investigate practices of the USPTO. A Government Accounting Office (GAO) report released June 2016 confirmed long-standing issues concerning patent quality control; describing that overwhelming volumes of patent applications have led to prioritization of turn-time over examination diligence. This trend has resulted in frequent grant of questionable or weak patents, fueling the excess litigation problem seen today:

> "GAO, which conducted its audit from 2014 to 2016, focused on how poor patents are contributing to the recent rise in litigation. Lawsuits in federal district courts over the illegal use of inventions have exploded in recent years, with 5,000 filed in 2015, up from 2,000 in 2007, the audit said..".
> "Just the threat of litigation can deter innovators from coming up with new products, GAO found."[47]

---

46 Dennis Crouch, USPTO's *Swelling Examiner Rolls*, Patent Lyo (2014), https://pate ntlyo.com/patent/2014/11/usptos-swelling-examiner.html (accessed Sep 5, 2017)

47 *Intellectual Property: Patent Office Should Define Quality, Reassess Incentives, and Improve Clarity*, Government Accountability Office (GAO), Report to Chairman, Committee on Judiciary, House of Representatives 1 (June 2016)

Firms attempting to innovate new products, particularly in computer technology, are facing interference from associated right holders; often leading to delays or abandonment of effort to avoid patent wars. De-incentivizing new product development in this manner runs counter to the fundamental objectives of the patent system and naturally carries negative economic and social implications.[48]

Another observation from the GAO report is that there are no clear criteria for even defining patent quality at the USPTO or otherwise. There has only been limited interpretation of language from the US Constitution and Patent Act:

> "The patent office 'does not have a consistent definition of patent quality that is clearly articulated… or fully developed measurable goals and performance indicators to guide and evaluate work towards the agency's quality goals,' GAO.."[49]

The USPTO largely concurred with findings of the GAO report in a formal response letter that expressed they continue to pursue improvement efforts.

C. 2016 GAO Report Findings

A chief concern expressed by GAO is that without a "consistent definition" for patent quality it is difficult to measure and monitor agency performance..as a result, it is hard for USPTO to define, measure, and work toward quality goals."[50] Furthermore, the USPTO describes a dilemma in which patent litigation attorneys prefer clearly defined claims, whereas rights holders tend to pursue more open-ended claims to widen applicability of their concept.[51]

Feedback from industry sources describe they feel that "time pressure" on examiners is a major contributor to compromised patent quality. This observation was verified from GAO's survey where an estimated 70% of examiners stated they have insufficient time to complete a proper examination with current volume demands.

---

48 *Id.* at 2
49 *Id* at 0
50 *Id* at 23
51 *Id* at 21

The report goes on to describe that determining prior art takes up most of the time required for examination. It does not help that applications are not required to show evidence of prior art search but only disclosure of any incidental knowledge of relevant art the applicant may have become aware of. GAO also notes that there is no limitation to the number of continuation requests that can be made by applicants. Therefore the only practical ends to an entered exchange are either a grant by the patent office or cessation by the applicant. [52]

Another concern is that examiners are graded based on the number of examinations they can complete each month. GAO estimates that 70% of examiners are pressured to circumvent lengthy formal exchanges with applicants. Examiners sense that the system prefers for them to approve a grant rather than engage in prolonged application reviews.[53]

D. *Analysis and Summary*

Criticisms of the USPTO contained in the GAO report are alarmingly comprehensive in that they describe fundamental flaws in both theoretical as well as operational aspects of the agency. Regarding the former, GAO highlights that the USPTO has not formulated a concept for patent quality itself never mind try to uphold it. Longstanding struggles with determining boundaries in exclusive rights ownership have become only more difficult with increased sophistication of technological development. Novelty and non-obviousness are becoming more subjective measures. And it hasn't helped that industry and political pressures have pushed the USPTO to sacrifice diligence for the sake of increased output.

It is also disconcerting to realize that these are not new problems. Another GAO industry survey report appearing twenty-three years prior paints a strikingly similar picture:

> "One company patent attorney said that the quality of examination has deteriorated significantly in recent years due to 'pendency pressures' and the lack of experience and knowledge of examiners in some technology fields. Another attorney, .. said that among the U.S., Japanese, and European patent systems, USPTO examination results are the 'most inconsistent.' .. one attorney said it is too easy to obtain patents on trivial or obvious inventions... Another

---

52 *Id* at 8
53 *Id* at 27

patent attorney noted that some patents are found to be valid even though they contribute minimally to the technology."[54]

Respondents reiterated that it was too easy to obtain patents for trivial concepts and that the patent office needs to better define "obvious" and return to a "no invention-no patent" policy. They also describe secondary undesirable consequences such as examiners manipulating lengthy procedures to compensate for lack of knowledge. For example, it was common for an examiner with insufficient understanding in a given subject matter to frivolously file an interference (pre-AIA, first to invent), sparking a dispute in order to indirectly derive explanation from ensuing exchanges between opposing parties. Lack of knowledgeable examination and excessive turn-times were similarly criticized for holding up product development due to apprehensions with conflicting matters being invisibly stuck in the "pipeline" at the patent office. [55]

The above list of significant problems reflect the technical challenges surrounding proper examination and granting of patent rights. Data from GAO suggests two fundamental vulnerabilities of patent quality that contribute to this situation. First is the technical challenge of assessing the patentability of proposed concepts where a) subjective criteria of "novelty" and "non-obviousness" are becoming increasingly difficult to interpret and b) a backdrop of growing and complex prior art adds to an already difficult search exercise.

Without more specific guidelines the task of assessing patent quality itself may become too subjective. This lack of measure has allowed the USPTO to escape full accountability for some time now, even in cases where there have been extensive error in patent examination and grant. Properly assessing patent quality without the establishment of more definite examination criteria has become increasingly unworkable. As will be illustrated with the *Apple* and *Wright* case studies, such shortcomings result in uncertainties that contribute to the size and frequency of patent litigation.

---

54 *Intellectual Property Rights: U.S. Companies' Patent Experiences in Japan*, Government Accounting Office, GGD-93-126, 14 (July 1993)

55 *Id.* at 15-16

IV. Patent War Today: Apple vs. Samsung

Apple's iPhone 3 disrupted the cell phone market in 2007. It brought a new touchscreen-driven user interface that made integration of features and navigating utilities on a mobile communication and computing device much easier than ever before. The series of *Apple vs. Samsung* cases beginning in 2010 represent the start of the "Smartphone Wars." Although many companies later became involved in associated litigation, this case was the central conflict, taking on a scale that stretched over several countries and jurisdictions. The narrative on these two companies and their legal confrontation has been the topic of films and popular periodicals.[56]

A. Background

1. iPhone vs. Galaxy

Top secret efforts on the iPhone began at Apple in 2004. Internal product teams had proposed the concept of a mobile phone with integrated computing in prior years, but Apple CEO Steve Jobs had been reluctant to move ahead due to apprehensions with existing market competition and dependence on third party cellular service companies. He also had technical concerns with achieving adequate internet connectivity on a mobile handset. A major shift in attitude occurred after Apple design director Jony Ive produced impressive smartphone mock-up units that showcased the "multi-touch glass" concept.[57] The company then moved ahead with smarthphone development.

By January 2007 Jobs announced the new iPhone product at the annual MacWorld show in San Francisco, CA. The cell phone establishment did not think the iPhone would be successful and for the first nine months of 2008, the iPhone did not gain much traction. As the market became more

---

56 Eichenwald, *supra*
57 *Id.*

aware of the iPhone and its features, demand increased to where Apple's production could no longer keep up with demand.[58]

Samsung, which was struggling in the smartphone market, understood it had to react to the iPhone sensation.[59] As the company worked on a new design, it began to resemble the iPhone itself both physically as well as in user interface features. In March 2010 the Samsung Galaxy S product was announced at the CTIA Wireless trade show. [60]

Despite Jobs' initial outrage at discovering the Galaxy S and its similarities to the iPhone, Apple pursued negotiations in hopes Samsung would agree to a license agreement. Then in March 2011 Samsung introduced a tablet computer resembling Apple's iPad2. Viewed as yet another "grand theft," Jobs reached a breaking point and launched a federal lawsuit against Samsung in a Northern California District Court for their infringement on both the iPhone and iPad. Apparently Samsung had been prepared as they responded with countersuits in Germany, Korea, Japan and the U.S. Related suits were eventually brought to Britain, France, Italy, Spain, Australia, and the Netherlands as well as federal court in Delaware and with the U.S. International Trade Commission (ITC).[61]

2. Patent Litigation

The subsequent global legal battle between Apple and Samsung has become famous for its size and scope and is associated with largest jury award for patent infringement in history (over one billion US dollars initially). The case has gone several rounds, spanning years and continents, and involved various patents introduced at each stage.[62] The following discussion mainly considers initial actions taken by the parties in trying to

---

58 *Id.*

59 *Id.*

60 *Id.*

61 *Id.*

62 Eingestellt von Florian Mueller, *Apple, Samsung provide final list of patents and accused products for California spring trial*, Foss Patents (Feb. 2014), http://www .fosspatents.com/2014/02/apple-samsung-provide-final-list-of.html (accessed Aug 27, 2017)

assert Smartphone rights as well as selected subsequent events that characterize the overall engagement.[63]

This starting round of the patent war was based on seven patents from Apple asserted against Samsung. Samsung's countersuit was based on five patents. The total of twelve patents are described below:[64]

Apple:
- 7,469,381: touchscreen actions, including dragging, pinch zoom, multi-touch, and bounce.
- 7,844,915: Application Program Interface (API) for a touch-sensitive devices.
- 7,864,163: touchscreen zoom and navigation methods.
- D618,677: design patent for physical structure of an early iPhone.
- D593,087: design patent for general outline of another early iPhone.
- D504,889: design patent for layout of an iPad tablet.
- D604,305: design patent for the "graphical user interface" (GPU).

Samsung[65]:
- 7,675,941: mobile phone 3G data transfer capabilities.
- 7,447,516: other mobile phone 3G capabilities.
- 7,698,711: MP3 playback technology for a mobile device.
- 7,577,460: a "communication terminal" for cellphone and camera data transfer
- 7,456,893: a method for indexing user's place in a gallery of images.

It is telling that Apple selected the above seven patents out of their portfolio of more than 1,300 patents in mobile electronics technology. This short-list, the majority of which are design patents, reflect a distillation to the iPhone's most noteworthy and appealing user features.[66] The "Total

---

63 Charles Mauro, *Apple v. Samsung: Impact and Implications for Product Design, User Interface Design (UX), Software Development and the Future of High-Technology Consumer Products*, PulseUX Blog (Dec 2012), http://www.mauronewme dia.com/blog/apple-v-samsung-implications-for-product-design-user-interface-ux-design-software-development-and-the-future-of-high-technology-consumer-produ cts/ (accessed Aug 25, 2017)
64 David Kravets, *Who Cheated Whom? Apple v. Samsung Patent Showdown Explained,* Wired (July 2012), https://www.wired.com/2012/07/apple-v-samsung-exp lained/ (accessed Aug 27, 2017)
65 *Id.*
66 Mauro, *supra*

User Interface and Experience" (TUX) engineering community has resultantly taken notice of this case. As one industry expert, Charles Mauro CHFP (Certified Human Factors Engineering Professional) has described, the selected patents from Apple cover largely artistic aspects of both the hardware and software yet, in combination with the user-interface, aims for a "whole greater than the parts effect."[67] The design patents cover the simple but elegant design of the iPhone form factor while the utility patents covered characteristic human interface features designed to ease access to internet resources such as email and web browsing. Samsung on the other hand, appears to have selected their patents "piece-meal" based on each claim's individual chances for broad application to mobile phone technology.[68]

In 2012 a California jury acknowledged Samsung's "copying" of the iPhone and awarded Apple $1.05 billion out of the $2.75 billion sought, but this was only the beginning of a long line of legal battles involving other patent infringement claims.[69] For example, Apple filed another lawsuit against Samsung in February 2012 on another set of patents maintaining that Samsung "has systematically copied Apple's innovative technology and products, features, and designs, and has deluged markets with infringing devices in an effort to usurp market share from Apple."[70]

B. Rulings

Despite the one billion dollar award for Apple in their first case, Samsung has been able to secure increasing amounts of market share as subsequent legal clashes have worn on. They have produced the "Apple-ish, only cheaper" Galaxy smartphone as well as derivative products such as tablets that leverage the same technologies and have gained market share and technical capability in the process.[71]

---

67 *Id.*

68 *Id.*

69 Apple Corporation v. Samsung Electronics. Ltd, No. 5:2011cv 01846 (N.D. Cal. Apr.15, 2011)

70 Tibken, *supra* referencing Apple Corporation v. Samsung Electronics. Ltd, No. 5:2012cv 00630 (N.D. Cal. Feb. 8, 2012)

71 Eichenwald, *supra*

For further insight into the extensive litigation, the following offers a selective review of associated rulings. The complex technical exchanges that were to follow also gave rise to fundamental legal questions associated with calculating appropriate damages for product infringement. These issues ultimately made their way to the U.S. Supreme Court.[72]

1. Patent Battles, Product War

Although it appears that the legal engagement between Apple and Samsung has finally drawn to a close with announcement of a settlement in June 2018, this development arrives only after years of costly international litigation. The seven-year confrontation has been characterized by a back and forth struggle that holds true to the popular "war" analogy. Both sides have had rounds of success and failure in the smaller battles confined to subsets of patents or jurisdictions. Some observers felt the first court decision against Samsung would have spelled their end in the smartphone market, but this has clearly not been the case.[73] Although Apple was able to obtain rewards that acknowledge the patent protection that surrounds their iPhone user experience, there were later cases when such patents were called into question and even invalidated. At the same time, although Samsung was often penalized for allegedly "copying" the iPhone and iPad, they were able to show that Apple did indeed infringe on some of their mobile technology patents. This record makes for lack of a clear victor in the smartphone war.

In line with this paper's analysis, this section intends to highlight three of the Apple patents that were found to be either invalid or unclear during subsequent litigation with Samsung. As with the list of original seven patents from the 2011 first filed case, the below utility patents reflect the "Total User Experience" (TUX) aspect of the iPhone product. One of the key questions to be considered later is the potential relationship between Apple's product-centric approach and recent trends in patent quality.

---

72 Samsung Electronics v. Apple Inc., No. 15-777 (S. Ct. Dec. 6, 2016)
73 Joe Mullin, *Apple's $120M jury Verdict against Samsung destroyed on appeal*, Arstechnica (Feb. 2016), https://arstechnica.com/tech-policy/2016/02/appeals-court-r everses-apple-v-samsung-ii-strips-away-apples-120m-jury-verdict/ (accessed Aug 27, 2017)

The first two Apple patents for consideration are 8,046,721 and 8,074,172 which describe the "swipe to unlock" and "auto-correct" spell check features respectively. Both patents were ruled invalid in February 2016 by the Court of Appeals for the Federal Circuit because claims "would have been obvious based on the prior art"; reversing the previous decision of infringement by the U.S. District Court for Northern District of California.[74]

Patent '721 primarily claims "A method of unlocking a hand-held electronic device, .. including a touch-sensitive display, the method comprising: ..continuously moving the unlock image on the touch-sensitive display ..wherein the unlock image is a graphical, interactive user-interface object ..." The Federal Circuit court opinion provides that the '721 patent is "directed to the 'slide to unlock' feature of the iPhone. As described in the specification, one problem with a portable device with a touchscreen is the accidental activation of features..cell phone manufacturers had long used 'well-known' procedures to prevent this, by locking the phone (i.e., not recognizing any touch inputs).. The '721 patent claims a particular method of unlocking. The user touches one particular place on the screen where an image appears and, while continuously touching the screen, moves his finger to move the image to another part of the screen."[75]

During the trial, Samsung provided two prior art references: a "NeoNode" N1 Quickstart Guide from 2004 and a presentation by "Plaisant" from a computer conference taking place in 1992. They argued these two references make Apple's '721 claims obvious.[76] Samsung's motion for "judgment as a matter of law" (JMOL) on invalidity was initially denied by the California District Court.

The NeoNode art provides an unlocking sequence for a touchscreen phone whereby the user "continuously" moves a finger on the surface of the screen. It also includes the feature of having text reading "Right sweep to unlock" on the screen to instruct users. Even Apple did not deny that this art captured essential elements of their claim, leaving only that Apple added a dynamic on-screen image whereas NeoNode did not call out for any such "moving image" response. Samsung argued that the second reference, the "Plaisant paper," provides this missing element with description of "six different touchscreen-based toggle switches to be used by

---

74 Apple Inc. v. Samsung Electronics Co. Ltd., No. 15-1171 (Fed. Cir. Feb. 26, 2016)
75 *Id.*
76 *Id.*

novice or occasional users to control two state (on/off) devices in a touch-screen environment." Two of these toggle switch representations, "slider toggle" and "lever toggle" shown below, closely resemble the "slide-to-unlock" feature of the iPhone.[77]

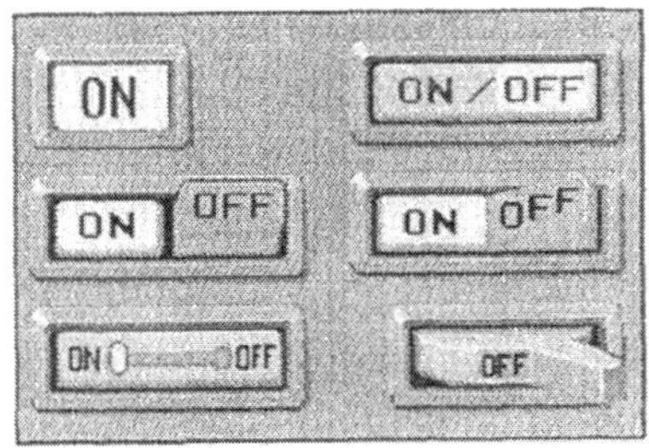

Figure 1: "slider toggle" on the bottom left and the "lever toggle" bottom right[78]

Together, this prior art invalidated Apple's '721 patent.

The second patent ('172, not to be confused with above '721) concerned Apple's claims for an automated spelling correction feature known as "autocorrect." This patent's primary claim is a "method, comprising: a..touch screen display: in a first area..displaying a current character .. in a second area of the touch screen .. displaying the current character string or a portion thereof and a suggested replacement character string.."[79]

As with the '721 patent, it describes a software-based interactive touch-screen feature. In this case the user can have spelling-correction suggestions appear on an intermediate scroll bar. Prior art was identified in U.S. patent 7,880,730 from Tegic Communications, LTD which includes a claim for a "..text entry system comprising .. an auto-correcting keyboard region comprising a plurality of the members of a character set, wherein locations having known coordinates in the auto-correcting keyboard region are associated with corresponding character set members.." Once again, Apple was not able to refute the similarity to this reference but in-

---

77 *Id.*
78 *Id.*
79 *Id.*

sisted that Samsung had nonetheless copied their recent implementation of this feature with the iPhone.[80]

In a third example, the Federal Circuit reversed findings of infringement by Samsung on Apple patent 5,946,647 based not on invalidity, but interpretation of the claims language. The District court jury had originally awarded nearly one-hundred million dollars to Apple on this patent after Samsung's request for JMOL was denied. Apple patent '647 describes a "tap-to-link" single-touch response feature that allows users to dial numbers or visit websites without cutting and pasting the link. The primary claim provides a "system for detecting structures in data and performing actions on detected structures, comprising: an input device..an output device..; a memory..including program routines including an *analyzer server* for detecting structures in the data, and for linking actions to the detected structures."[81]

Neither Samsung nor Apple had pursued formal interpretation of what comprised an "analyzer server" so the Federal Circuit resorted to an "ordinary meaning" interpretation of their own. Citing another case, Motorola, 757 F.3d at 1304, the court had "construed 'analyzer server' to mean 'a server routine separate from a client that receives data having structures from the client.'" In other words, the term "server" denoted a client-server configuration where a host resource is providing processing capability to a remote client. Therefore Apple's view of the "analyzer server" simply being "a program routine(s) that receives data, uses patterns to detect structures in the data and links actions to the detected structures "– and that "the analyzer server *need not be 'separate from a client'* " was rejected because it ignored the commonly held meaning by those familiar with the art.[82]

Apple's expert witness attempted to retrofit the operation of iPhone's tap-link function into the refined definition by emphasizing the critical software resided on a different portion of the phone's memory and processor and thus could be considered a separate "server" in the established sense. The court rejected this argument stating "this testimony is not sufficient evidence to allow a jury to conclude that the Samsung software met the 'analyzer server' limitation .. client-server computing is a *distributed*

---

80 *Id.*
81 *Id.*
82 *Id.(emphasis added)*

computing model in which client applications request services from server processes."[83]

2. Section 289 Damages

As if technical aspects of patent interpretation and determining infringement between Apple and Samsung were not complex enough, the magnitude of the judgment awards being generated by juries over various trials soon led to fundamental questions regarding how these values were calculated. For example, in March 2013 U.S. District Court Judge Lucy Koh ordered "a new trial to recalculate some of the damages in the case, striking four-hundred and fifty million dollars off the original judgment against Samsung."[84]

Further questions on damage calculations ultimately made their way to the U.S. Supreme Court with a key decision provided in December 2016.[85] The decision reversed and remanded a prior judgment by the U.S. Federal Circuit Court of Appeals which based damages on total sales enjoyed by Samsung's infringing product line. Leading technology companies such as Google and Facebook had lobbied the Supreme Court to hear Samsung's appeal due to concerns that the sizable judgments made against it "will lead to absurd results and have a devastating impact on companies because of the implications of how patent law is applied to technology products such as smartphones."

In the written summary of the unanimous Supreme Court opinion, Judge Sotomayor first described that "Section 289 of the Patent Act makes it unlawful to manufacture or sell an 'article of manufacture' to which a patented design or a colorable imitation thereof has been applied and makes an infringer liable to the patent holder 'to the extent of his total profit.' ..35 USC. § 289 " It goes on to describe how a jury awarded Apple about four-hundred million dollars in damages according to "Samsung's entire profit from the sale of its infringing smartphones." The Federal Circuit rejected Samsung arguments for reduced damages "because the relevant articles of manufacture were the front face or screen rather than the entire smartphone" and that "components of Samsung's smartphones were

---

83 *Id.(emphasis added)*
84 Tibken, *supra*
85 Samsung Electronics v. Apple Inc., No. 15-777 (S. Ct. Dec. 6, 2016)

not sold separately to ordinary consumers and thus were not distinct articles of manufacture."[86]

The Supreme Court reversed this Federal Circuit decision and instead held that "in the case of a multi-component product, the relevant 'article of manufacture' for arriving at a § 289 damages award need not be the end product sold to the consumer but may be only a component of that product." § 171(a) of the Patent Act permits "a design patent that extends to only a component of a multi-component product.." Finally, Judge Satomayor provides "because the term 'article of manufacture' is broad enough to embrace both a product sold to a consumer and a component of that product, whether sold separately or not, the Federal Circuit's narrower reading cannot be squared with § 289's text." [87] The case was remanded for calculation of reduced damages.[88]

This decision should have a significant impact on future high-technology litigation in that it bounds potential damage awards for infringement. Many stakeholders have expectedly welcomed the Supreme Court ruling."[89] Nonetheless, these events provide a dramatic example of the tremendous losses that may result from not properly bounding associated exclusive rights in the first place.

C. Analysis

Although the Apple vs. Samsung litigation saga has apparently come to a close, it will take more time to understand the full impact it may have on future technology disputes. In the meantime, there are numerous indications that have been made thus far. Discussed below are notable observations, which include the scale of the litigation, trends in patent protection strategy, and the apparent state of the current patent system.

---

86 Samsung v. Apple , 15-777 at 1
87 *Id.*
88 Crum, *supra*
89 *Id.*

1. Colossal Legal War

The *Apple vs. Samsung* patent war has taken on a grand scale, lasting more than seven years, costing more than a billion dollars and spread as wide as four continents. Some contend that even though it has been one of the "bloodiest corporate wars in history," Apple "may have won legal battles but still lost the war." A source near Apple reports "that the endless fighting has been a drain on the company, both emotionally and financially." [90] During the last year of his life, Steve Jobs spoke of Apple's patent-violation lawsuit against Google, whose Android mobile operating system enabled Samsung's smartphones: "Our lawsuit is saying, 'Google, you (expletive) ripped off the iPhone, wholesale ripped us off.' Grand theft.'" [91] Perhaps most will identify with Steve Jobs' outrage and agree that Samsung has largely succeeded in mimicking a revolutionary product concept introduced by Apple.

Still, questions remain as to how much of the iPhone was truly protectable from competitors from a patent standpoint and whether the iPhone itself relied on technologies held by Samsung and others. Each party was prepared with plentiful "ammunition" in the form of vast patent portfolios but were selective with their patents when it came to trial. Although this approach may have been strategic, especially in the case of Apple, Judge Lucy Koh had also forced the companies to limit the number of claims set forth in order to ease the process for an overwhelmed jury.[92] Future cases may not have such limits set.

This paper takes the view that the scale of litigation was indeed excessive. Although Apple had some initial success with the 2012 U.S. District Court ruling, the follow-up litigation probably indicated they were starting to throw "good money after bad." Neither Apple nor Samsung achieved complete success in their legal war. In South Korea infringement was found on both sides. In Japan a court did not accept an Apple claim. In Germany, there was a sales ban on the Galaxy Tab 10.1 due to its close match in appearance and function to Apple's iPad2. In Britain, a court

---

90 Eichenwald, *supra*
91 Diamond, *supra*
92 Paul R. Gugliuzza, *Patent Trolls and Preemption*, 101 No. 6 Virginia Law Review 1579 1590 (October 2015)

found for Samsung, stating that its tablet was "not as cool" as the iPad so would not mislead customers.[93]

2. Invention vs. "Cool" Product

Industry analysis of this case suggests that TUX design will become more important as individual features become less separable from accumulating technology. In light of the Apple case, TUX analyst Mauro asserts:

> "Smart companies going forward will work with their IP counsel to frame patent applications and related litigation toward protecting the total user experience of their products. But the road to an IP strategy like Apple's that focuses on the total user experience may not be an easy one. The current legal system works in exactly the opposite direction by requiring inventors to slice up their products into many features .."[94]

Nonetheless, Apple's strategy of clustering TUX patents appears to have met with some success. Continuing along this path may afford companies more opportunity to fortify their trade dress claims with related patent filings. As developments in TUX become more dramatic and distinguished, companies may begin attempts to patent such combinations "to protect the ..'whole' of their user experience solutions across all relevant customer touchpoints."[95]

The prospect of leveraging patent rights into trademark-like protection is an unintended and detrimental consequence of such a trend. Should identification of a "cluster of patents that combine to drive high levels of user engagement" become an invention itself? TUX developers appear excited that Apple has taken first steps to doing just that.[96] These concerns are discussed further below.

3. Questionable Patents

In addition to revealing Apple's TUX patent clustering strategy, the case also highlights fundamental questions of whether these types of software

---

93 Eichenwald, *supra*
94 Mauron, *supra*
95 *Id.*
96 *Id.*

patents should qualify for utility patent protection in the first place. Legal analysts have suggested that both Apple and Samsung incorporated "intellectual property that should never have been patented." [97] Author and legal scholar from UC Hastings College of the Law, Robin Feldman, commented on the favorable ruling for Apple in 2012 with:

> "Regardless of the outcome of the trial, we might want to step back and consider whether society should be granting such powerful rights so easily. Are the features at issue here really deserving of so much protection? .. On the whole, the trial is one more indication of a patent system that has lost its bearings, with litigation rather than innovation leading the way."[98]

The iPhone was undoubtedly an impressive and groundbreaking product from a consumer perspective but whether it deserved the enormous transactional costs associated with utilizing legal resources for prosecution and litigation in this way is a long term question that society will have to answer. Given the descriptions of many of the Apple software patents in contention, it does not appear reasonable for the companies to have spent well over one billion dollars and corresponding public resources to try and secure absolute command of the smartphone market through such means. As the 2016 GAO report indicates, the abstract and ubiquitous nature of software seems to have only added to the patent quality problem.[99]

Transactional costs are not limited to litigation. In an academic article from Berkeley Law School appearing in 2012 author Thomas H. Chia provides:

> "Smartphone companies are amassing enormous patent portfolios in order to remain competitive against a rival's patent portfolio...This patent strategy is analogous to the military tactic of mutually assured destruction. However, continually amassing patents under a mutually assured destruction strategy may not be financially sustainable or desirable from the perspective of technological innovation."[100]

The USPTO is already overwhelmed with applications and wrestling with quality issues. The flood of questionable software patent applications due to this "amassing" only adds to difficulties.

---

97 Kravets, *supra*

98 *Id.*

99 GAO-16-490 at 0

100 Thomas H. Chia, *Fighting the Smartphone Patent War with RAND-Encumbered Patents*, 27 Berkeley Technology Law Journal 209, 214 (2012)

V. Patent War Yesterday: Wright v Herring-Curtiss

A. Background

In December 1903, more than 100 years prior to the iPhone, the Wright brothers demonstrated their working Wright Flyer heavier-than-air prototype aircraft. Attempts at human piloted aircraft had been ongoing for several decades in the form of primitive balloons and gliders. These prior aircraft lacked control and thus served limited utility. Wilbur and Orville Wright then developed a breakthrough tri-axis control system by incorporating a "wing-warping" mechanism into aircraft design. By twisting and shaping the wing, a pilot can maintain balance and directional control during flight much like a bird adjusting the contour of its wings. Achieving such equilibrium had proved elusive until this point. This breakthrough ushered in the age of modern aviation which today utilizes the associated "aileron" to achieve directional control on fixed wing aircraft.[101]

The move from wing warping to use of ailerons as well as a host of other substantial improvements to the Wright Flyer concept were achieved early on by Glenn Curtiss, inventor and engine designer. Curtiss recognized an opportunity to apply his technical capabilities and know-how from motorcycle engine design to aircraft. He entered the aircraft business and started producing superior prototypes in hopes of securing government and private interest. After hearing of his methods of simplifying wing shape control, the Wright brothers quickly confronted him with a lawsuit. They felt strongly that their patents covered any variations to wing surface alteration lending to aircraft control and thus Curtiss' design for ailerons and other components became their intellectual property. Curtiss did not agree with the Wrights' claims and continued to innovate new aircraft designs while evading enforcement of their issued patents.[102] A contentious period followed where the Wrights suffered substantial interruption to their business while Curtiss also struggled to continue improvements on aircraft design in the midst of legal confrontations. As with *Ap-*

---

101 Lawrence Goldstone, Birdmen: The Wright Brothers', Glenn Curtiss, and the Battle to Control the Skies 41 (2014)
102 *Id.* at 124

ple vs Samsung, these events have become the topic of historical debate with a central question being whether the *Wright vs Herring-Curtiss* patent war disrupted what otherwise would have been a more rapid and efficient evolution of American aircraft design.[103]

B. Analysis

Some analysts feel that the Wrights had become too focused on securing profitability after their initial success with their Wright Flyer prototype aircraft As attorney and columnist Matt Levine describes:[104]

> "Rather than take advantage of their legal monopoly by developing, promoting and selling the airplane, they kept it under wraps, refusing for many years even to show it to prospective purchasers. However, while refusing to devote any effort to selling their own airplane, they did invest an enormous amount of effort in legal actions to prevent others, such as Glenn Curtis, from selling airplanes."[105]

Opponents of the patent system point to *Wright vs. Herring-Curtiss* as yet another example of how innovation is inhibited rather than encouraged under such a system.

It is helpful to describe certain aspects concerning the patent system as it existed in the early 1900s to obtain added perspective on the role of patent quality in large scale litigation. Firstly, the patent office at the turn of the century appears, at least for aviation claims, to have set forth a more rigorous examination than what exists today. Initial attempts by the Wrights to patent their aircraft structure were met with refusals from the U.S. patent office. Their first application submitted in March 1903 was rejected for a host of reasons including drawings that were "inadequate," claims perceived to be "vague and indefinite," as well as suggestions that their work was already covered by at least six pre-existing patents.[106] To top it all off, the examiner suggested the Wrights' concept was "a device

---

103 Matt Levy, *Yes, The Aviation Industry Was Nearly Derailed by the Wright Brothers' Patent*, Patent Progress 67 (Jan 2015) https://www.patentprogress.org/2015/01/12/yes-aviation-industry-nearly-derailed-wright-brothers-patent/ (accessed Aug 25, 2017)
104 *See* U.S. patent 821,393
105 Michele Boldrin & David K. Levine, Against Intellectual Monopoly, 21 (dklevine.com 2004)
106 Worrel, *supra*

that is inoperative or incapable of performing its intended function;" in other words, he did not believe it would really work. Apparently it did not help that the patent office had been flooded with applications from "cranks" claiming aviation patents that were not plausible or substantiated.[107] In any case, it is notable that despite having less formal procedures than today, the patent office reacted to these conditions by qualitatively raising the standard on demonstrated utility for incoming applications concerning aviation.

A second point, obscured by limited historical account, is the question of how much the Wrights actually contributed to the centuries old efforts at achieving powered, manned flight. The Wright brothers had been fascinated with flight from a young age and made efforts to track the efforts of other famous aviation pioneers. A primary example is German engineer Otto Lilienthal who in 1889 "produced the most advanced study ever written on the mechanics of flight, *Der Vogelflug als Grundlage der Fliegekunst* – 'Bird-flight as the Basis of Aviation.'" [108] Wilbur Wright followed Lilienthal's work and was inspired by him to pursue aircraft development.

Wright tracked and communicated with other notable pioneers in aviation such as Octave Chanute, a French American engineer who completed extensive research into high-lift airfoil designs.[109] Chanute had published a compilation of his technical articles in 1894 under the title *Progress in Flying Machines*. In his assessment for fixed-wing "aeroplanes," he concluded that the "problem of the maintenance of the equilibrium is now, in my judgment, the most important and difficult of those remaining to be solved .." [110] There is record of the Wrights referencing these prior works and the Wright 821,393 patent operates upon the principle of resolving the equilibrium challenge described by Chanute.[111]

Not only is there the question regarding contributions occurring before an invention, but also how to "parcel out" inventions that arise post-grant. The primary claims by the Wrights in their '393 patent state broad terms:

> 1. In a flying-machine, a normally flat aeroplane having lateral marginal portions capable of movement to different positions above or below the normal

---

107 Goldstone, supra at 30
108 *Id. at 3*
109 *Id. at 12*
110 *Id. at 14*
111 *Id.*

> plane of the body of the aeroplane, such movement being about an axis transverse to the line of flight, where-by said lateral marginal portions may be moved to different angles relatively to the normal plane of the body of the aeroplane, so as to present to the atmosphere different angles of incidence, and means for so moving said lateral marginal portions, substantially.."

The essential segments of language, repeated in many of the subsequent claims, centers upon the aeroplane's (or "wing's") ability to "be moved to different angles .. so as to present to the atmosphere different angles of incidence." In the Wright Flyer aircraft prototype used to demonstrate this method, a mechanism of pulleys was used to flex the wings of the aircraft in order to deflect oncoming airflow and steer the entire aircraft.

Glenn Curtiss was a talented and proficient mechanical engineer experienced with developing powerful and light-weight motorcycle engines. He was initially drawn to aviation when realizing the benefit his light-weight engines could provide to aircraft.[112] As he started building entire aircraft on his own, he came up with an alternative to the wing warping approach used by the Wright Flyer. Instead of warping the entire wing of the aircraft, Curtiss instead placed controllable hinged tabs near each wing-tip (compare Figures 2 and 3). This modification not only dramatically simplified aircraft design and improved mechanical reliability, but also offered better steering control compared to the full wing warping employed by the Wrights. This wing tab, now known as an "aileron," remains an essential component of aircraft design today.

---

112 Goldstone, *supra,* at ixxx

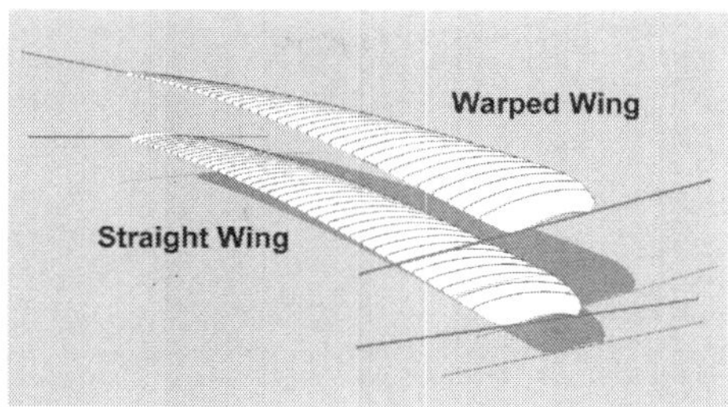

Figure 2: Illustration of Wright concept of "wing warping"[113]

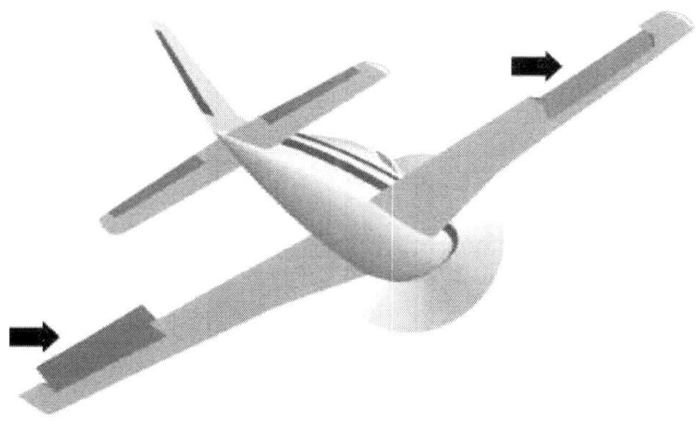

Figure 3: Ailerons (moveable) with fixed straight wing of modern aircraft[114]

The Wrights pressed on to have their patent granted in 1908 and later followed up with impressive public displays of their working Wright Flyers. However, as Curtiss and other interested parties joined in on aircraft development, the Wright brothers became so consumed by the litigation that they started to fall behind on further research and development.[115] Still, courts had recognized their achievement and ultimately held their patents

---

113 Wright-Brothers.org, http://www.wrightbrothers.org/History_Wing/Wright_Story /Inventing_the_Airplane/Wagging_Its_Tail/Wagging_Its_Tail_images/1902-Glider-wings-compared.jpg (accessed Sep 5, 2017)

114 Precision Graphics, http://cf.ydcdn.net/1.0.1.80/images/main/A5aileron.jpg (accessed Sep 5,2017)

115 Goldstone, *supra*, at 203

valid and infringed. Furthermore, the courts considered their progress "to be of a pioneer nature entitled to having their claims given the broadest interpretation" therefore would cover Curtiss' ailerons as well as wing warping.[116] Curtiss and other parties viewed their improvements to aircraft design as distinctive so remained defiant. The conflict was settled only after Assistant Navy Secretary Franklin Roosevelt in 1917 "pressured the rivals to allow unrestricted production of airplanes for the war effort," bringing the Wright patent war to a close.[117]

---

116 Worrel, *supra*
117 Sean Trainor, *The Wright Brothers: Pioneers of Patent Trolling*, Time (Dec. 2015), http://time.com/4143574/wright-brothers-patent-trolling/ (accessed Sep. 3, 2017)

VI. Synthesis and Analysis

As described, this paper aims to examine the role of patent quality in contributing to patent wars and generally increased litigation seen in recent years. As a baseline, Chapter II provided overview on legislative origins of the US patent system. Chapter III summarized major concerns brought up in a recent GAO audit of the USPTO; many of which are associated with patent quality. In Chapter IV, the *Apple vs. Samsung* smartphone litigation was reviewed and analyzed as a modern example of a patent war whereas Chapter V described the *Wright vs. Herring-Curtiss* patent war occurring almost one hundred years prior. These complementary perspectives have been provided to help illustrate the constant challenges with maintaining an effective patent system.

This chapter provides corresponding synthesis and analysis of these perspectives beginning with comparison of original intents with current practices of the U.S. patent system followed by a review of supplementary data to the GAO (2016) report. The aspect of utility of invention is then considered before comparison of the *Apple* and *Wright* patent wars. Finally, a list of primary challenges facing the US patent system is compiled based on this analysis.

A. Drift from Historical Basis

As provided Chapter II, Framers of the U.S. Constitution and legislators from the first Congressional proceedings relied considerably on the example set by Britain for establishing a patent system. They aligned with the British precedent to set up an effective, low-cost registration-based patent system.[118] The requirements outlined in first Congress' H.R.10 emphasized utility and reliance on public feedback as a method of governing declared exclusive rights. Apart from the savings in cost, there was already recognition that any examination process presented a daunting, unfeasible task of research and evaluation.[119] Still, in 1836 the United States resorted

---

118 Walterscheid, *supra,* at 37
119 *Id.* at 98

to an examination-based patent system due to loss of control over abusive and fraudulent filing activities. Circumstances had deteriorated to the point where applicants were copying already existing patents in order to obtain a formal letter grant for use in intimidating unwitting "infringers." By 1835 license revenue from such fraud was estimated at approximately half a million dollars per year.[120]

But how had matters reached such a point? The answer appears to rest in the fact that the newly established U.S. was a vast geographical territory.[121] Given the limited communication and transport technology of the day, this would have made timely mass communication quite difficult. A first consequence is that much of the population was not aware of the dishonest practices surrounding patent issues until it was too late. More fundamentally, lack of effective mass communication disabled the "public notice" function intended by the Patent Act of 1793. The country was "an enormous place and publication of advertisements in Philadelphia ..New York and even Boston would not give adequate notice across the country of the existence of ..particular patent application."[122] As such, one may consider that the registration procedure was never truly implemented under such circumstances.

Resultantly the Patent Act of 1836 introduced the examination-based system which formed the basis of the U.S. patent system of today. Establishment of the USPTO and growing needs for legal protection of technology have probably introduced more cost overhead than the Framers were able to imagine; perhaps even calling into question whether the patent system is still offering benefit to society.

In addition to introducing enormous cost, today's examination-based patent system has also fallen short in maintaining the emphasis that early Congress placed on utility of invention. In the late 19th century much of the enthusiasm surrounding the patent system was derived from expectations that it would encourage development of machines with capabilities that would make up for the shortages in manpower relative to abundant land resources enjoyed by the new nation. Furthermore, American leadership had its sights on greater industrialization as a long term goal.[123]

---

120 Kenneth W. Dobyns, The Patent Office Pony: A History of the Early Patent Office 97 (1997)
121 *Id.* at 43
122 Walterscheid, *supra,* at 98
123 Dobyns, *supra* at 43

Growing influence from industry and capacity limits for patent examination have worked to diminish patent quality and traditional notions of utility with it.

In sum, the modern patent system appears to have drifted far from the early vision for the U.S. patent system as described in the U.S. Constitution, H.R.10 and the Patent Act of 1793. The move from registration to examination has introduced burdens that were not part of the original "low-cost" British model for a patent system. Furthermore, reliance on public disclosure and discourse as a mechanism for governing patent recognition has been replaced by an overwhelmed examination process that introduces significant delays in publication with arguably no significant increase in legal certainty. Finally, subjective standards on utility have been lowered to allow too many weak patents. Recent improvements such as third party reviews and patent office review boards reflect some modest steps back towards a system of self-regulation but it is not clear whether these formalized methods are sufficient for addressing future challenges.

B. *Long-standing Patent Quality Concerns*

The GAO (2016) report on the USPTO's performance describes a disconcerting array of both fundamental and operational problems. Additionally troubling is that this report reflects a state of affairs representing at least the last forty years. Problems with patent quality and increased litigation are long-standing issues.

In their aptly titled book from 2008, "Patent Failure," economic and legal authors James Bessen and Michael J. Meurer delve into an assessment of the U.S. patent system in relation to the tangible property ownership scheme after which it is modeled. They observe that the patent system is falling far short of this ideal model due to four reasons:[124]

- *"fuzzy boundaries"*: uncertainties with interpretation of claims language that is so complex that there is "no reliable way of determining patent boundaries short of litigation"

---

124 James Bessen & Michael J. Meurer, Patent Failure: How Judges, Bureaucrats, and Lawyers Put Innovators at Risk 10-11 (2008)

- *"public access to boundary information"*: delays and maneuvering "hide language for many years.." thus adding uncertainty and risk to R&D investment
- *"scope of rights"*: during litigation claims are often widened or narrowed beyond what was intended by patentee adding more uncertainty
- *"patent flood"*: current USPTO criteria such as non-obviousness and operational practices are not working well

The authors describe that these issues have led to a tripling in patent litigation over about a thirty-six year span (see Figure 4).[125] These points resemble the 2016 GAO report; which itself was initiated due to a doubling of patent litigation between 2007 and 2015.

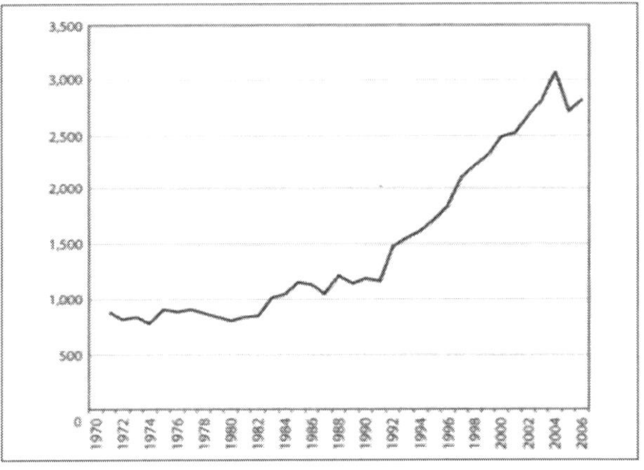

Figure 4: U.S. Patent Lawsuits Filed in District Courts[126]

Bessen and Meurer focus on the term "patent notice" as a parameter measuring how well the patent system mimics land ownership. This parameter appears to embody both scope of property rights and awareness of those rights by society. In other words, they envision that patent rights be as clearly defined as a fenced area of land clearly marked with "do not enter" signs on all sides.

---

125 *Id.*at 17
126 *Id.* at 122 (taken from Administrative Office of the U.S. Courts; John L. Turner)

> "..the genius of a property rights system is that it relies on .. judicial discretion as *little* as possible … Without clear notice, no property system can work well and the result is excessive disputes… Indeed, Duffy (2000) writes, 'The quality of an authoritative claim interpretation depends not on its fidelity to some abstract ideal of interpretation, but on its *predictability.*'" [127]

Whether an equivalency to the land ownership model can ever be truly realized remains a debate, but nonetheless it provides a target standard.

This paper takes the term "patent notice" to effectively mean the same thing as "patent quality." Ironically, it comes down to interpretation of the language being used for these commonly used terms. Arguably higher patent quality would result in greater certainties regarding patent validity and scope, which in turn would provide the improved boundaries and patent notice that Bessen and Meurer seek.

Similar to GAO (2016), "Patent Failure" points out that software patent litigation has been a particularly problematic area whereas subject matters in chemical and pharmaceutical products have not exhibited such increases in litigation.[128] This correlates to the abstract nature of software claims which have tested the definition of patentable material in well-known cases such as *Bilski* and *Alice v Mayo*. Adjustments from case law have apparently not been enough to address the greater challenges posed by such abstraction.[129]

These same struggles of the patent system have been documented by other government research. For example, in June 2004 a Congressional subcommittee on Courts, the Internet and Intellectual Property held a hearing to obtain industry feedback on proposed patent opposition procedures designed to cut down on invalid patent grants. Guest speakers included distinguished IP professionals from high-profile corporations such as Google and Genentech.[130] During opening comments, state of Virginia representative Rick Boucher provided that although an "interference" reexamination was an option for challenging a patent any time after grant, it required new and compelling prior art to be introduced, as well as other strict formalities making the method effectively inactive. [131]

---

127 *Id.* at 235

128 *Id.* at 21

129 *Id.* at 22

130 *Patent Quality Improvement: Hearing Before the Subcomm. on Courts, the Internet, and Intellectual Property*, 108th Cong. 39 (2004)

131 *Id.* at 3

During the hearing Mr. Karl Sun, Senior Patent Counsel for Google, Inc. provided a presentation where he highlighted many of the same concerns that would be mentioned eight years later in the GAO (2016) report. Amongst the issues raised were observations on how the USPTO incentivized patent examiners "according to a point or 'count' system that encourages patent issuance." He stressed that changes to the system have to acknowledge the actual conditions facing the patent office:

> "Reforms need to recognize and address the practical realities of the patent system, including the burgeoning rate of patent filings, an overworked and understaffed examining corps, and the ex parte process.."

Sun goes on to describe that increased third party challenges should be enabled and not restricted to narrowed patent office criteria such as novelty and non-obviousness.[132]

The realities alluded to by Sun and others are not limited to the United States. Worldwide, patent offices are facing challenges with high rates of patent invalidation. For example, in a recent paper examining legal certainty for patent holders in Europe, Professor Dr. Christoph Ann of Technische Universität München (TUM) provides there "is no disputing the fact that the success rates of nullity suits against German patents and for EP (European) patents valid in Germany are considerable" and that this trend "is not new, but has been more or less unchanged for more than at least 50 years."[133] Ann cites a 2014 study which revealed that nullity actions on software and telecommunications patents "led to almost a rate of 60% total invalidations for the period 2010-2013. Approx. 30% of patents were partially invalidated. And only a good 10% were upheld." [134] In Japan, the rate of patent invalidation by trial in 2006 was as high as 70%. Although this rate has been driven down by improved review processes, the average invalidation rate over the following nine years was approximately 40-50%.[135]

---

132 *Id.* at 39
133 Christoph Ann, *Patent Invalidation and Legal Certainty - What Can Patent Holders Expect?* SSRN (July 5, 2016) 16, https://ssrn.com/abstract=2804992 (accessed Aug 29, 2017)
134 *Id.* at 6
135 Atsushi Sato, *Japan Patent and Trademark Update,* TMI Associates, Issue 7 (July 2017), https://www.tmi.gr.jp/wp-content/uploads/2017/07/jptu-vol.7.pdf (accessed Sep 5, 2017)

Finally, in 2016 Notre Dame law school Professor Steve Yelderman expressed the benefits of "patent challenge" to competition law. Referring to the 2011 Leahy-Smith America Invents Act which introduced the new opposition proceedings he states:

> "One theory that is specific to patent disputes is that they present an opportunity to mitigate the harms to competition imposed by individual patents. On most accounts, the purpose of having patent system is to reward invention through time-limited bequests of market power. According to this theory of the benefits of patent challenges, such cases can reduce or eliminate the patent holder's market power, stemming the harms to competition that might otherwise flow from an overbroad or invalid grant."[136]

In effect, these additional administrative reviews provide "a golden opportunity to mitigate the costs of having a patent system." [137] He also stresses that there is "public interest in free competition" that "is not necessarily represented by any of the parties to a particular dispute." [138] Patent challenges therefore not only resolve specific mistakes but also lend to gained public confidence in the system that increases incentives for future inventors.[139]

C. Unwritten Rule on Utility

Language regarding promotion of the "useful arts" originates with the U.S. Constitution and corresponds most directly with "helpful and value trades" given the context in which it was developed.[140] The term "useful arts" has been reiterated in subsequent patent legislation and has worked to shape the evolution of patent law ever since. In order to consider the implications intended by this requirement, especially relative to modern-day practices, it is helpful to obtain some additional historical perspective.

Beginning with H.R.10, section 3, petitions for patent are specified for "any new art, manufacture, engine, machine, invention or device." [141] The majority of these terms are associated with objects that can benefit from

---

136 Stephen Yelerman, *Do Patent Challenges Increase Competition?*, 83 4, The University of Chicago Law Review 1946 (2016)
137 *Id.* at 1952
138 *Id.* at 1953
139 *Id.*
140 Walterscheid, *supra* at 51
141 *Id.* at 435

performance improvements as demonstrated in the late 18th century. For example, "engine" suggests a powerplant used for running equipment or perhaps a transport device such as the steamboat being developed at the time. "Manufacture" referred to mass production such as that enabled by the cotton gin. These key words suggest a basis upon which quantification can be used as a tool to distinguish one idea from the next. For example, a machine such as Eli Whitney's cotton gin was shown to double the yield of raw cotton production.[142] In this way it may be drawn that the Founders envisioned patents to represent inventions that similarly provide measurable improvement to the state of a trade or industry. "Progress of the useful arts was contemporaneously understood to mean promoting the development of manufacturing." [143]

This directive to improve America's position in manufacturing is reflected in a statement made by George Washington in 1790 during an address to Congress: "a free people ought not only to be armed,..their safety and interest require that they should promote such manufactories, as tend to render them independent from others for essential, particularly, for military supplies."[144]

Although today's U.S. patent code inherits the foundational language surrounding "usefulness" from early legislation, there has been surprisingly little elaboration on this requirement in the over two centuries since. Although entitled a "utility patent" there is no detailed description for a "utility" requirement. According to USPTO guidelines, a "utility patent is issued for the invention of a new and useful process, machine, manufacture, or composition of matter, or a new and useful improvement thereof.."[145] Guidelines for examining utility provide only that a "credible" and "specific" or "well-established" utility should be included in the specification of the patent application.[146] Per 35 U.S.C. section 112, the specification portion of a patent application requires only that the applicant provide a

---

142 Joan Brodsky Schur, *Eli Whitney's Patent for the Cotton Gin*, National Archives (2016), https://www.archives.gov/education/lessons/cotton-gin-patent (accessed Sep 5, 2017)

143 Walterscheid, *supra* at 146

144 Walterscheid, *supra* at 148

145 USPTO website, *Types of Patents,* https://www.uspto.gov/web/offices/ac/ido/oei p/taf/patdesc.htm (accessed Sep 5, 2017)

146 USPTO website, Synopsis of Application of Utility Guidelines with Examples, https://www.uspto.gov/ip/rules/proposed/utility-synopsis.jsp (accessed Sep 5, 2017)

description of the invention "in such full, clear, concise, and exact terms as to enable any person skilled in the art" to "make and use the same." Legal scholars point out that section 112, in addition section 100 of the patent code which defines patentable subject matter, provide a mechanism for ensuring some credible utility aspect to the filed invention.[147] Still, the limited treatment of utility in United States code and USPTO guidelines results in little practical barrier for applicants when it comes to this aspect of usefulness of invention.

Adding to this bearing is the relatively scarce U.S. case law on the matter of utility. Scholars point mainly to the renowned Joseph Story, Associate Supreme Court Justice and Dane Professor at Harvard Law School and his opinion from *Lowell v. Lewis*, (Court, D. Massachusetts, 1817 15 F.Cas. 1018) which "set forth the contours of the utility requirement which persist today."[148] The defendant in this case tried arguing that the patent for a competing pump design was not valid because the plaintiff could not prove that his invention "is of general utility; so that in fact, ..it must supersede the pumps in common use.. and must be, for the public, a better pump..." [149] Judge Story flatly disagreed with this view, instead providing that the Patent Act of 1793 intended only to block any inventions that may be "frivolous or injurious to the well-being, good policy, or sound morals of society" and that the word "useful" is used in "contradistinction to mischievous or immoral."[150] Judge Story emphasized that utility criteria should not impose any restrictions on the flow of incoming ideas because frivolous concepts would naturally and "silently sink into contempt and disregard." Notably, this opinion was formed while the patent system was still in the "age of registration" established by the Patent Act of 1793.

Given the dramatic changes in technological and legal landscape since 1817, one should question how well Judge Story's position aligns with modern circumstances. Patent Law Professor Martin J. Adelman provides:

"This sense of 'practical' or 'beneficial' utility is an all-or nothing proposition: Either the claimed invention possesses utility or it does not..does Justice Story's assertion that no harm befalls the public if a patented invention pos-

---

147 Martin J. Adelman, U.S. Patent Law class (lecture), Munich Intellectual Property Law Center (Apr. 2017)
148 Taken from Martin J. Adelman, MIPLC U.S. Patent Law Casebook 91 (4t ed. 2016)
149 Martin J. Adelman, MIPLC U.S. Patent Law Casebook 91 (4t ed. 2016)
150 *Id.*

sesses limited utility remain correct? Doesn't the public suffer the burden of lengthened examination times when notoriously overworked patent examiners must allocate scarce resources towards the extended consideration of worthless technologies?"[151]

This paper contends that in light of the documented challenges facing the modern patent system, the answers to above questions are "no" and "yes" respectively.

D. *Comparing Apple and Wright Cases*

The stories behind the *Apple* and *Wright* patent wars have some interesting parallels as well differences which help expose long-standing challenges facing the patent system. The cases are compared here.

In terms of similarities, both cases were fueled at least in part by a deep-seated rivalry stemming from what was perceived as theft of personal property. The land ownership model appears to successfully take hold with respect to this human dimension. The Wrights and Steve Jobs both felt their inventions were stolen and were seemingly driven as much by a moral sense of justice as concern for material losses. How much of a role such emotion plays is difficult to ascertain but it seems likely that human factors only aggravate such volatile situations. One can at least draw the conclusion that it is in the interest of society to establish property systems that facilitate fair and expedient resolution in such disputes. Any violations in land usage such as trespassing would be dealt with swiftly by law enforcement and other government officials. The delays and uncertainties that the patent system presented in each case provided conditions where emotions could fester and hence contribute to protracted resource-consuming litigation.

Both cases also dealt with breakthrough products emerging as the world was on the cusp of disruptive technological change. In the 1900s the industrial revolution was well underway with inventions such as the light bulb and gasoline engines beginning to gain traction. There was already much research activity underway with aviation, most of which concentrated on balloon aircraft due to considerable difficulties with heavier-than-air flight.[152] In the case of smartphones, the emergence of the information age

---

151 *Id.* at 92
152 Goldstone, *supra* at 7

58

was the disruptive technological backdrop. In both cases there was naturally a "burgeoning" of invention and business pursuit as industry players and innovators struggled to stake their claims for the future. Such circumstances present a stress-test to the patent system, which is tasked with "parceling" out property rights commensurate to achievement for each patent applicant. The increased volume of patent applications and dynamic nature of new technology make the already daunting task of examination all the more difficult during such periods.

Examining the differences between *Apple* and *Wright* can begin with consideration of the U.S. patent office in 1903 versus 2010. As mentioned, Wilbur Wright had a difficult time getting his patent granted due to apprehensions with revealing required data to the patent examiner. In line with early practices of the patent office, examiners routinely expected to see substantial supporting evidence of invention whether it be in the form of technical reports, testimonies, or working models. The Wrights' reluctance to display their aircraft cast doubt on their claims; indicating the patent office at this time maintained a rigorous, albeit subjective, standard for utility on patent grants. This approach is contrasted with the practices already described by GAO (2016) where patents are granted too easily.

Therefore there are two extremes being represented in the contemporaneous patent office practices in each of these patent war cases. One can view the *Wright* scenario representing a period of "under-patenting" where the patent office may have disregarded legitimate concepts due to emphasis on supportive data on claims. In contrast, the modern era has provided an "over-patenting" environment where too many bad patents are passing examination due to criteria that are diminishing in the face of increased time and resource pressures placed on the patent office.

These differences in patent system practices correspondingly led to different approaches to litigation. The difficult standard on utility patents at the time of *Wright* had them rest all litigation on their '323 patent which described how to achieve aircraft equilibrium in fairly broad terms. Once their patent was granted, courts provide the wide interpretation of claims afforded by "principle" patent status. This is in contrast to the "arms race" approach used by large corporations such as Apple and Samsung facilitated by the patent system of today. Furthermore, the complexity and high degree of overlap occurring in high-congestion subject matters such as smartphone technology led Apple to successfully pursue a clustered "user experience" approach to legal protection that some argue represents spillover of patents into trade dress rights. Again, these are circumstances that arguably have resulted from the patent quality challenges that have been exhaustively documented over the last several decades.

As a sidenote, both cases occured outside the foundational registration-based system described in Chapter I. Both faced challenges with having patent examination proportionately allocate exclusive rights under these "under-patenting" and "over-patenting" conditions. Still, probably due to its proximity in history, the *Wright* case reflects a system that lies closer to original intentions described by the first sessions of U.S. Congress. The aforementioned strict regard for claims-supporting evidence exhibited by the patent office in 1903 appears to take greater measure at upholding the "new and useful" requirement as understood in the late 18th century.

In summary, the *Apple* and *Wright* cases illustrate that irrespective of historical placement, a primary challenge of any patent system is indeed the appropriate identification and bounding of patentee exclusive rights. With *Apple* one sees invention being effectively diced and diluted down into hundreds of patents many of which have no classic inventive substance; i.e., low patent quality. These high numbers inevitably result in complex entanglements with market competitors leading to patent war. On the other hand, with *Wright* one sees invention being reserved for only the most dramatic and substantial demonstrated achievement, effectively disregarding legitimate contributions made by other parties. This scenario can also be considered a display of low patent quality in that the disclosure was not properly bounded. Both scenarios led to patent war. As will be described in the next chapter, it is suggested that proper "tuning" of a patent system to avoid such extremes is likely unattainable with an examination-based system. Instead, the USPTO should consider a newly enabled implementation of the original patent registration framework depicted in H.R.10 and the Patent Act of 1793.

E. Net Challenges

Despite overwhelming support for a federal patent system amongst the Founders there existed skeptics such as Thomas Jefferson who voiced "ambivalence concerning the merits and efficacy of the American patent system" and apprehensions with the challenging task of "parceling" exclusive rights to inventors in a fair and consistent manner. [153]

The daunting challenges of patent examination were indeed recognized by government officials as early as 1790. After a brief attempt at instituting the process, there was a return to registration after a "dawning recognition by the members of the patent board, and particularly by Jefferson, that they simply had insufficient time to properly carry out the tasks assigned to them.."[154] The board was overwhelmed with applications, leading to "frustrating" delays for inventors. Unfortunately this scenario sounds all too familiar today.

As Jefferson took part in preparing the Patent Act of 1793 he built upon concepts introduced with H.R.10. The registration system would require applicants to file a notice in "every District Court of the United States" as well as "three times in some one Gazette of each of the said Districts."[155] His concern over "trifling" invention submissions likely played a role in devising this procedure for public disclosure. [156] These activities indicate that the Founders were well acquainted with the challenges of proper examination in determining divisions in inventor exclusive rights.

This proper division of intellectual property has been shown to depend on patent quality because high quality patents establish legal certainty. By definition, high quality patents can survive opposition challenges and describe clear boundaries of ownership. The property model described by Bessen and Meurer reflects this conventional academic thought on the matter. What the recent GAO report and a host of other studies have shown however, is that consistent quality is not being achieved with today's costly ex-parte application and examination procedure.

Adding more question to the tremendous expense of the examination process is the fact that the vast majority of issued patents are never even implemented. In a 2007 journal article discussing the "bad patent" problem, law professors Lichtman and Lemley provide:

> "a..growing number of 'patent trolls' today (are)..using patents on obvious inventions quite literally to tax legitimate business activity..What to do? One tempting idea is to increase PTO funding, making possible more rigorous upfront screening..but the drawback is that most of the money would be wast-

---

153 Walterscheid, *supra* at ix
154 *Id.* at 195
155 *Id.* at 202
156 *Id.* at 201

> ed..most patents lie dormant after issuance..They are lottery tickets..Money spent perfecting these documents..is money thrown away." [157]

Thus the drawbacks of full patent examination are two-fold: unrealistic expectations for completing thorough examination and massive amounts of wasted effort processing inconsequential "dormant" patents.

In summary, the net challenges facing today's patent system can be reduced to two "classic" problems recognized over 200 years ago:

– *Subjective patent criteria:* definitions and standards for novelty, non-obviousness, utility, and enablement have varied throughout history due to changing landscape as well as limitations with language interpretation leading to inconsistent results and reduced legal certainty.

– *Unrealistic patent examination process:* determining patent validity in a closed examination-based process has always been an insurmountable and wasteful prospect. Only a fraction of patents are challenged. Examiners do not have time or resources to complete a proper examination anyway, and are actually incentivized to grant issues. This situation leads to delayed publications and weak patents which also undercuts legal certainty, inviting opportunity for more litigation that inhibits innovation.

Given these problems the question becomes: what other ways besides ex-parte examination can be used to achieve patent quality? As suggested, a modernized version of the Patent Act of 1793 offers at least one option.

---

157 Lichtman and Lemley, *supra* at 48

VII. Proposals

Below are respective proposals for addressing the two root problems identified from the analyis contained in the previous chapter. A "utility parameter" is introduced as an added entry for patent content in order increase objectivity in determining patent value as well as scope. Such parameter is to be incorporated with a return to a registration-based patent system that leverages the latest capabilities in information technology.

A. The "Utility Parameter"

Chapter VI, section C provided that original meaning for the utility requirement for patents emphasized measurable improvements to manufacturing. In 1817 Judge Story did not want to impose any requirement that a patent "must have" improved utility over existing methods but only that it did not introduce any detrimental or immoral subject matter. He did so in order avoid imposing unnecessary restrictions on incoming ideas, instead relying on an assumption that any patents lacking in utility would naturally "sink" into obscurity. Unfortunately, instead of "sinking" away, bad patents continue to surface amongst the sea of growing litigation described by GAO and others.[158]

One should also consider that during early U.S. history, utility of an invention was more easily recognizable. Again, the cotton gin had doubled the rate of textile manufacturing. In contrast, modern notions of utility have been obscured by greater competition, market influence, technical complexity and uncertainty. This situation has led to many "weak" patents being issued on what amounts to obvious or slight design variations.

This paper proposes that introducing a "utility parameter" as a formal, albeit unverified, entry on patent applications would inject a needed measure of objectivity in what has become an excessively subjective exercise of claims interpretation. The utility parameter would simply require the applicant to *quantify* the significance of their invention by whatever means

---

158 *Id.*

he or she feels is most suitable for capturing the advantage that the invention offers. For example, if an inventor developed a new fuel injector design for engines that resulted in increased vehicle range, the inventor can specify how many more kilometers of travel can be obtained from a given amount of fuel for a particular size and weight of vehicle based on either calculated estimates or actual test data. Ideally this improvement would be supported by attaching such reports but it would not be required. The primary purpose for the utility parameter is to assist in bounding a patent by revealing substantially more about the nature and result of the intended invention itself. Therefore, it would also help determine whether there is truly any "equivalence" with a contending patent claim. The utility parameter purported by the applicant would be tested only in the event the patent is formally challenged. Such test would also consider the extent to which the patentee has actually demonstrated said utility parameter, in order to discourage empty or inflated figures.

Although many applicants may already include content resembling a utility parameter in their specification and claims, there is currently no requirement to do so. This proposal only requires that the utility parameter include a quantification of benefit and be presented in clear and understandable language as a formality of the patent application. There would be no binding standard for a minimum utility beyond what is suggested by existing U.S. patent law. The utility parameter intends only to provide a missing "measuring stick" for use in an evaluation process that is otherwise restricted by often ambiguous standards for novelty and non-obviousness; hence helping to more quickly eliminate weak patents and "fuzzy boundaries" on claims.

B. *"High-Tech" Patent Registration*

As described in Chapter VI, Section A, the major logistical problem facing the patent registration system in 1793 was lack of patent notice communication capability. Furthermore, there was a general lack of understanding with regards to patent issues and abuses that were taking place at the time. In today's communication and information age these problems simply no longer exist.

1. Description

It is proposed that with use of modern information technology, the USPTO can now access the public support once sought by the Founders to assist in governing patent issues. An online registration-based patent system would leverage public expertise and manpower that would dwarf the efforts of current examination proceedings. These efforts would provide greater illumination of the patent landscape, leading to improved anticipation of patent strength.

It is important to note that this proposed online system is not intended to provide a legal determination on patent validity built on consensus. Instead it enables expression of a perceived public value or strength in association to a given patent. It is simply an electronic registry database and public forum that promotes expedited disclosure and the accumulation of public feedback. The gathered commentary would effectively provide a "word on the street" reading that can assist the public as well as stakeholders in their assessment of patent positioning and strength. It would not legally determine what is a valid patent, but instead assist in identifying what is a "valued" patent.

Users of the online system would be registered and verified by the USPTO patent registry website. Relevant user and demographic data such as associations with certain companies or industries would be collected for each user account. Users would then be able to leave named or anonymous commentary on a moderated "message board" occurring for each registered patent. Users would use these message boards in much the same way as many popular social media sites such as Yahoo, Google, and Facebook.[159] Individuals may leave questions or comments regarding each patent. To avoid patentees being inundated with commentary, moderator support as well as advanced consensus identification utilities such as "voting up" options can be used. Voting items up or down would help identify the most pressing questions or comments from the general public which the patentee can then respond to online. Notably the USPTO already employs an online utility that resembles this scheme for gathering ideas from

---

159 Chris Dixon, *Why Google Succeeded Where Other Search Engines Failed,* Business Insider, (2011) http://www.businessinsider.com/accurate-contrarian-theories -2011-5?IR=T (accessed Sep 7, 2017)

the public on how to improve the Manual on Patent Examination Practices (MPEP).[160]

Applicants would file online and have their registered patents published after a formality check that should take no more than sixty days to process. Timely disclosures and publication benefit the research and development community by minimizing the number of applications hidden in the "pipeline" at any one time.

2. Compatibility with Existing Systems

Installation of the proposed online patent registration system would be minimally disruptive to the existing legal infrastructure. All existing legal proceedings including formal post-grant review would remain intact. Patent law would maintain existing criteria such as novelty and non-obviousness, introduce new entries such as the "utility parameter," yet eliminate the requirement for formal examination of patent filings. Instead, applications would be rapidly posted to the online database. The online registry would be equipped with adjoining search and communication forum functionality. In addition, it would be designed to process filing fee payments and facilitate an efficient formalities-only incoming check by the USPTO. This online repository would also enable the attachment of data and media files that support stated claims. An advanced search function that updates with the latest image and algorithmic search capabilities would also be provided to users. Powerful computer sciences such as artificial intelligence and block-chain crytography can be harnessed to help the USPTO manage an increasingly vast volume of time-sensitive data. These advances would be applicable to all aspects of the patent process; from search, to prosecution, and, as necessary, during litigation.

Electronic patent registration would be disruptive only as far as eliminating the burdensome and wasteful examination process being attempted today. The existing infrastructure of courts, agencies and legal services will of course still be needed but these resources would be used much more efficiently and effectively. The USPTO would undergo downsizing but maintain a contract examiner resource pool through establishment of supplementary private agencies. Full-time examiners would be able to tru-

---

160 USPTO, Ideascale, https://uspto-mpep.ideascale.com/ (accessed Sep 7, 2017)

ly hone their skills and help improve search algorithms when they are no longer rated on 'count' of patent grants per month, but rather thoroughness of examinations, limited to important and high-potential subject matters as described below.

3. Agency Examination Option

As a supplemental option, a professional examination report by the USP-TO or government-approved third party agency may be provided, at a premium fee, for those seeking a stronger indication of patent value. The patentee is free to elect whether or not to post findings of such a report. As with any non-legal opinion, such report would not serve to provide determination of validity. It would only reflect additional steps beyond nominal processing taken on the part of the patentee to verify strength of claims.

The above formal agency review option may appear to reintroduce patent examination that favors well-financed corporations but selective third-party examination input is not likely to overcome the self-regulation enabled by low-cost public registration. Professional assessments would be discouraged from offering binary determinations on patent status. Instead, they would provide a "strength rating" such as a percentage likelihood of patent validity in a third-party challenge. Like any other opinion, this assessment would be open for questioning if posted publicly. Furthermore, the online database would track these assessments against results from actual litigation or challenge. Hence, an "accuracy rating" can be generated for each agency providing a measure of competition and quality control that escapes the USPTO today. To add, a fixed-capacity USPTO with private agency supplementation would provide a more flexible and cost-effective examination resource.

4. Benefits

The "open book" approach of online patent registration should accomplish far beyond even what the Founders had sought with the newspapers of their day. With internet-enabled advanced information management resources, relevant patents would undergo a virtual "townhall" review process where the general public could weigh-in on strength of the claims being set forth.

This high-visibility, crowd-sourcing scenario would result in a database that can be used to dramatically reduce litigation and avoid patent wars. Greater real time access to the patent landscape would enable more "pre-game" analysis for those considering post-grant review, litigation or other formal patent challenges. The consensus of opinion contained in such a registry would provide a virtual examination process that should dissuade questionable claims and frivolous legal actions. It should also encourage private settlement. Public commentary on patentee claims regarding novelty, non-obviousness, and the utility parameter would provide a supplemental cross-check to private analysis parties may be pursuing in parallel. Furthermore, by "laying out all their cards" sooner, rival companies are provided better opportunity to propose patent pool or standards-essential patent agreements which can work to avoid potential patent wars.

An online patent registry would also provide judges and attorneys means to become rapidly acquainted with a given subject matter by browsing relevant message boards associated with any case at hand. In this way, industry participants as well as the general public will have a chance to have their voices heard without having to surmount the formalities or exposure of a formal patent challenge or litigation.

5. Risks and Unknowns

Some may argue that an online registration system will invite similar as well as new types of abuses as seen between 1793 and 1836. As described, the problems taking place after the Patent Act of 1793 were due mainly to a lack of adequate communication and information regarding patent notice and alerting the public to abuses. In today's internet age, these problems would be eliminated. Anyone across the world with internet connection would be able to see and comment on the latest patent filings within seconds of issue. Furthermore, unscrupulous individuals can no longer hide behind a document with the Presidential Seal as they did in the early 1800s. Any new attempts at intimidation or abusive methods would be quickly exposed given today's resources.

Although there remain risks with any such reform, there is also possibility of unknown benefits. An online registry may produce yet unpredicted advantages such as the emergence of public *reputation* as contributing self-governing factor. For example, some may still be concerned with companies "flooding" the registry with worthless patents as an intimidation tactic. Firstly, employees may be reluctant to be personally named as inventors on such patents as they will no longer be able to point to the USPTO as having fully concurred with their application; this would make the inventor solely responsible for outlandish or false claims that are later exposed. Furthermore, such companies would probably be called out on the public forum anyways. Repeated actions such as flooding or filing of weak or obvious patents can be made apparent with data filtering and information ranking options easily worked into an online database. Again, any company can choose to challenge public findings in formal proceedings, but the backdrop provided by online consensus should reduce these actions to only the most deserving disputes.

6. Summary

The above provides only a rough sketch of the framework and potential benefits of restoring original U.S. patent registration principles through modern means. There are hosts of other factors to consider alongside such a reform. Other elements to be incorporated may include reduction of patent terms, increases in filing fees, and other procedural adjustments. The focal point however, remains to be the leveraging of public participation and advanced data management tools to achieve a crowd-sourced virtual examination process that minimizes governmental expense while effectively maintaining high patent quality standards. Such a system would lead to increased legal certainty that works to encourage innovation. Theoretical application of this proposed system to the *Apple* and *Wright* scenarios is provided in the concluding chapter.

VIII. Conclusion

In closing, this paper has provided a historical perspective on origins of the U.S. patent system along with review of patent quality and two well-known patent wars. This information reveals a persisting quality crisis with patents on most subject matters. This crisis corresponds to a drift away from founding constructs of the U.S. patent system; a foundation that emphasized usefulness, disclosure and publication before grant of exclusive rights. An effective restoration of these founding principles is now possible using technology that is available today. This paper concludes with theoretical application of proposed reforms to the *Apple* and *Wright* cases and final remarks.

A. Revisiting Apple and Wright

Below is a theoretical exercise that applies the proposed utility parameter and online registration system from Chapter VII to the *Apple* and *Wright* cases. The purpose is to illustrate how such a system may have helped avoid or reduce the extent of these patent wars.

With *Apple vs. Samsung* we see that Apple devised an assertion scheme based on clustering of "user experience" patents, most of which covered the physical design and graphical icons on the iPhone. The "utility parameter" may have provided both direct and indirect effects that could have distinguished the product in a more substantial and meaningful way than what essentially amounts to electronic trade dress. A contemporary study completed by Google titled "The New Multi-screen World" has revealed a "staggering shift in user behavior toward engaging with smartphones first as their primary entry point for a wide range of tasks that have critical business impact...now 65% of all tasks involving 'Searching for Info' start on the smartphone."[161] No doubt Apple's iPhone has caused this migration to mobile usage due to the features that it highlights such as on-screen manipulation with a user's fingers. But whereas the current content

---

161 Mauro, *supra*

of patents focuses on showing "how" users are able to use their fingers to engage on-screen images, the utility parameter would reinforce the "why" behind such a feature. For example, for Apple's two-finger zoom, they may have elected to enter utility parameter data which captures how much more quickly users are able to search for data or check email compared to conventional scroll and select methods used on existing phones. Such data places focus on the true appeal of the iPhone, increased utility, rather than the artistic and fluid features than enable that utility. This utility is reflected in the findings of the Google "Multi-screen" report. The utility parameter would have more prominently displayed this distinction, cutting down on long, subjective arguments on whether an infringing product looked "cool" enough to be mistaken for an iPhone.

Indirectly, the virtual examination aspect of the proposed registration system would have helped counter the stockpiling strategy employed by both companies by "devaluing" questionable software claims. Furthermore, by referring to online patent registration data, Apple may have approached Samsung on patent pooling proposals to pre-empt confrontations on upcoming products such as the iPhone and iPad. For example, Apple may have recognized the relevance of Samsung's 3G patents earlier and negotiated a patent pooling agreement. They could have negotiated favorable terms before revealing the iPhone, making it out of reach from Samsung due to this pre-placed agreement. A number of other hypothetical outcomes can be speculated but the point is that increased focus on product utility and visibility could have helped avoid or at least shorten the smartphone war between Apple and Samsung.

In the case of *Wright v Herring-Curtiss* we find an example of the conundrum facing most "principle" patents which disclose sweeping claims on an enabling technology. This conundrum was represented by the conflict between the Wright "wing-warping" method of lateral aircraft control and Curtiss' more efficient aileron construction. It is an example that goes to the heart of the question regarding how to "parcel out" inventor rights. Here again a utility parameter may have helped break the theoretical stalemate between what were two good ideas.

To illustrate this point, the following analogy is offered. Consider someone "inventing" a single pole for use as a bridge to cross over small rivers. The original inventor can quantify benefit in terms reduced cost by arguing boats would no longer be required to traverse the waterway, or reduced time and distances for travel. A second party then designs a ladder style bridge which incorporates two poles connected by a series steps thereby eliminating the need for careful balance as travelers traverse over it. Under current standards the first party will argue that the ladder bridge idea from the second party is an "obvious" derivation of the first party's original idea. The second party will argue that their bridge is much less dangerous and easier to use for an average traveler thus represents a new invention. A debate would ensue as courts try to resolve whether a ladder is really just two poles set next to each other or a new concept all together. With the utility parameter, the second party would now be able to document quantifiable benefit in a mode they deem most relevant. For example, they would be able to run a study that compares the average transit time of a group of individuals when using the ladder style bridge against use of the single pole. They could also collect statistics on the rate of falls or missteps on their design versus the single pole. This data could be provided as an attachment under the utility parameter entry. In the event of litigation, courts could then use this additional resolution to help determine whether the new ladder design deserves an exclusive right of its own.

In similar fashion, the difference between Wright's wing warping and Curtiss' aileron would have been better documented with use of a utility parameter. Although an aileron operates under a similar principle as wing warping, the amount of simplification it presents to aircraft design is immense. Warping an entire wing multiplies the number of connections and control mechanisms required from the cockpit to the wing, imposes substantial limitations to aircraft material options, and compromises flight control authority. It is no wonder that Curtiss' aileron remains an essential part of aircraft design today. These advantages could have all been more readily captured if each inventor was forced to contemplate a utility parameter at filing. In this way, the values for both Wright and Curtiss would have been recognized earlier and dealt with accordingly; likely through a cross-licensing agreement.

To reiterate, the utility parameter is not proposed as a binding criterion. Its purpose is to inject a measure of objectivity that may help overcome the subjective criteria of novelty and non-obviousness in many cases.

Finally, the registration system would have likely forced the Wright Brothers to demonstrate their Wright Flyer much sooner than they actually did. Wilbur Wright was apparently reluctant to showcase his design until it was "locked-up" with a patent grant. Firstly, the lowered barrier for filing with registration would have increased the risk that another party would file a similar concept sooner. Secondly, the data from flight tests would become a greater component of substantiating the registered patent. Both of these factors should have inspired the Wrights to disclose their idea more quickly while continuing to focus on developing and improving their aircraft design. Instead, they were consumed with lengthy exchanges with the patent office and subsequent litigation.[162]

B. Looking Ahead

As provided in the introduction to this paper, noted economist A.T. Hadley once stated: "a patent system, if *properly* guarded, seems to be thoroughly justified by its results." Over one hundred years prior, Thomas Jefferson, acting as one of the first examiners of U.S. patents proposed a shift to registration due to "insufficient time to *properly* carry out tasks assigned to them."[163] These congruent observations reveal that patent quality lies at the core of a properly functioning patent system. This quality relies on establishing a degree of confidence on the value and reach of any given patent issue. It has become abundantly clear that the closed examination process cannot establish this required level of confidence today and that this task will only grow more difficult with time.

Once again, this understanding reaches beyond the U.S. patent system. As Professor Dr. Ann highlights in his 2016 paper on patents and legal certainty:

> "Examiners who feel all too secure here may want to consider the well-known quote by *Bob van Benthem*, the EPO's first president: 'I mean . , ., that the examiner, who is sitting at his desk outside the practice, should show some modesty. He should not be a specialist. Even auditors who have a great deal of practical experience inevitably lose contact with the practical artisan problems, if they have only spent a few years in the office.'".[164]

---

162 Goldstone, *supra*

163 *See* note 154

164 Ann (2016), translated with www.translate.google.com, original quote *"Ich meine . . ., dass der Prüfer, der abseits der Praxis an seinem Schreibtisch sitzt, eine gewisse Bescheidenheit an den Tag legen sollte. Er sollte sich nicht als Spezialist aufspielen. Sogar Prüfer, die große praktische Erfahrung hinter sich haben, verlieren unweigerlich in gewissem Grade den Kontakt mit den praktischen handwerklichen Problemen, wenn sie erst einige Jahre im Büro verbracht haben"*

Patent invalidity rates in Europe, Japan and the United States have been cause of ongoing concern and debate despite the tremendous resources being expended on examination each year.

The USPTO needs to acknowledge that the current patent examination process is no longer feasible. An alternative, robust and comprehensive method for ensuring patent quality is needed to avoid further loss of confidence in the system. In his 2012 article, Judge Posner goes on to echo much of today's sentiment stating "that there appear to be serious problems with our patent system, but almost certainly effective solutions as well, and that both the problems and the possible solutions merit greater attention than they are receiving."

This paper has proposed that introducing a utility parameter with return to a registration-based patent system as originally envisioned by the Founders offers a solution to these serious problems. Registration that leverages modern information technology enables the USPTO to "share the load" of patent value assessment with the public and would better represent the scheme outlined by one of America's first patent examiners, Thomas Jefferson. Jefferson based his framework on long term concerns for a newly formed nation. And for years after his tenure, he continued to emphasize the importance of properly determining which ideas were "worth to the public" of an exclusive patent right. Who better to enlist for this task than the public itself?

List of Works Cited

Cases:

Samsung Electronics v. Apple Inc., No. 15-777 (S. Ct. Dec. 6, 2016)

Apple Inc. v. Samsung Electronics, No. 15-1171 (Fed. Cir. Feb. 26, 2016)

Apple Corporation v. Samsung Electronics. Ltd, No. 5:2012cv 00630 (N.D. Cal. Feb. 8, 2012)

Apple Corporation v. Samsung Electronics. Ltd, No. 5:2011cv 01846 (N.D. Cal. Apr. 15, 2011)

Constitutions:

U.S. Const. art. I, § 8, cl. 8

Statutes:

35 U.S.C. § 100-103

Leahy-Smith America Invents Act of 2011, Pub. L. No. 112-29, § 125, Stat. 284 (2011)

U.S. Patent Act of 1836, 5 Stat. 117 (1836) taken from EDWARD C. WALTERSCHEID, TO PROMOTE THE PROGRESS OF USEFUL ARTS at 497-509

U.S. Patent Act of 1793, 1 Stat. 318 (1793) taken from EDWARD C. WALTERSCHEID, TO PROMOTE THE PROGRESS OF USEFUL ARTS at 479-483

U.S. Patent Act of 1790 1 Stat. 109 (1790) taken from EDWARD C. WALTERSCHEID, TO PROMOTE THE PROGRESS OF USEFUL ARTS at 463-468

Legislative Materials:

Intellectual Property: Patent Office Should Define Quality, Reassess Incentives, and Improve Clarity, GOVERNMENT ACCOUNTABILITY OFFICE, GAO-16-490, Report to Chairman, Committee on Judiciary, House of Representatives (June 2016)

Patent Quality Improvement: Hearing Before the Subcomm. on Courts, the Internet, and Intellectual Property, 108th Cong. (2004)

Machlup, Fritz, *An Economic Review of the Patent System: Hearing Before the Subcomm. on Patents, Trademarks, and Copyrights,* 85 Cong. 2 (1958)

H.R. 10, 1st Cong. (1789) taken from EDWARD C. WALTERSCHEID, TO PROMOTE THE PROGRESS OF USEFUL ARTS at 433-439

Books:

O'REGAN, G., PILLARS OF COMPUTING: A COMPENDIUM OF SELECT, PIVOTAL

Technology Firms (2015)

Bottomley, Sean, The British System during the Industrial Revolution 1700-1852, 28 Cambridge IP and Information Law 53 (2014)

Goldstone, Lawrence, Birdmen: The Wright Brothers', Glenn Curtiss, and the Battle to Control the Skies (2014)

Bessen, James & Meurer, Michael J., Patent Failure: How Judges, Bureaucrats, and Lawyers Put Innovators at Risk (2008)

Boldrin, Michele & Levine, David K., Against Intellectual Monopoly, (dklevine.com 2004)

Walterscheid, Edward C., To Promote the Progress of Useful Arts: American Patent Law and Administration, 1798-1836 (1998)

Dobyns, Kenneth W., The Patent Office Pony: A History of the Early Patent Office (1997)

Gordon, Thomas T. et al., Patent Fundamentals for Scientists and Engineers, 7 (3d ed. 1995), https://books.google.de

Periodicals:

Yelderman, Stephen, *Do Patent Challenges Increase Competition?*, 83 4, The University of Chicago Law Review pg, (2016)

Diamond, Arthur M., Seeking the Patent Truth: Patents Can Provide Justice and Funding for Inventors, 19 N.3 The Independent Review 325, (2015)

Graham, Stuart & Vishnubhakat, Saurabh, *Of Smart Phone Wars and Software*, 27, American Economic Association 67, (Winter 2013)

Chia, Thomas H., *Fighting the Smartphone Patent War with RAND-Encumbered Patents*, 27 Berkeley Technology Law Journal 209, (2012)

Worrel, Rodney K., *The Wrights Brothers' Pioneer Patent*, 65 American Bar Association Journal 1513, 15xx (1979)

Articles:

Eichenwald, Kurt, *The Great Smartphone War*, Vanity Fair (May 2014), https://www.vanityfair.com/news/business/2014/06/apple-samsung-smartphone-patent-war (Aug 29, 2017)

Crum, Rex, *Supreme Court throws out Apple's $399M win in Samsung patent fight*, Mercury News (Dec. 2016), http://www.mercurynews.com/2016/12/06/supreme-court-throws-out-apples-399m-win-in-samsung-patent-fight/

Whittemore, Lauren E., *U.S. Government Accountability Office Releases Two Reports on the United States Patent and Trademark Office and a Survey of USPTO Examiners*, Fenwick and West LLP (Aug 2016), http://www.lexology.com/library/detail.aspx?g=b49734c2-6e59-4970-8354-8b3ff5e0d853

Davis, Ryan, *GAO Says Time Pressure At USPTO Leading To Poor Patents*, Law360 (July 2016) https://www.law360.com/articles/819570

Rein, Lisa, *Patent Lawsuits Swell and Watchdog Says the Government is to Blame*, WASHINGTON POST, (July 2016), https://www.washingtonpost.com/news/powerpost/wp/2016/07/20/patent-officetktk/?utm_term=.be6d9769eecb

Broussard, Mitchel, *Apple Loses Appeal in Samsung Case: Two Patents Ruled Invalid, $120 Million Verdict Overturned*, MACRUMORS (Feb. 2016), https://www.macrumors.com/2016/02/26/apple-samsung-appeal/

Mullin, Joe *Apple's $120M jury verdict against Samsung destroyed on appeal*, ARSTECHNICA (Feb. 2016), https://arstechnica.com/tech-policy/2016/02/appeals-court-reverses-apple-v-samsung-ii-strips-away-apples-120m-jury-verdict/

Trainor, Sean *The Wright Brothers: Pioneers of Patent Trolling*, Time (Dec. 2015), http://time.com/4143574/wright-brothers-patent-trolling/

Oatman-Stanford, Hunter, *Let There Be Light Bulbs: How Incandescents Became the Icons of Innovation*, COLLECTOR'S WEEKLY (July 2015) https://www.collectorsweekly.com/articles/let-there-be-light-bulbs/

Matt Levy, *Yes, The Aviation Industry Was Nearly Derailed by the Wright Brothers' Patent*, PATENT PROGRESS (Jan 2015), https://www.patentprogress.org/2015/01/12/yes-aviation-industry-nearly-derailed-wright-brothers-patent/

Nocera, Joe *Greed and the Wright Brothers*, NY TIMES (Aug 2014), https://www.nytimes.com/2014/04/19/opinion/nocera-greed-and-the-wright-brothers.html?_r=2

Tibken, Shara *Apple v. Samsung patent trial recap: How it all turned out*, CNET (2014), https://www.cnet.com/news/apple-v-samsung-patent-trial-recap-how-it-all-turned-out-faq/

Von Florian Mueller, Eingestellt , *Apple, Samsung provide final list of patents and accused products for California spring trial*, FOSS PATENTS (Feb. 2014), http://www.fosspatents.com/2014/02/apple-samsung-provide-final-list-of.html

Hendricks, Drew, *7 Simple Ways You Can Protect Your Idea From Theft*, FORBES (Nov. 2013), https://www.forbes.com/sites/drewhendricks/2013/11/18/7-simple-ways-you-can-protect-your-idea-from-theft/#7af8b02b1f86

Mauro, Charles *Apple v. Samsung: Impact and Implications for Product Design, User Interface Design (UX), Software Development and the Future of High-Technology Consumer Products*, PULSEUX BLOG (Dec 2012), http://www.mauronewmedia.com/blog/apple-v-samsung-implications-for-product-design-user-interface-ux-design-software-development-and-the-future-of-high-technology-consumer-products/

Grosse Ruse-Khan, Henning, *Options Within the IP System to Promote Minor Innovations*, WIPO Regional Seminar (Sep 2012), MAX PLANCK INSTITUTE FOR INTELLECTUAL PROPERTY AND COMPETITION LAW, http://www.wipo.int/edocs/mdocs/aspac/en/wipo_ip_kul_12/wipo_ip_kul_12_ref_t4b.pdf

Kravets, David *Who Cheated Whom? Apple v. Samsung Patent Showdown Explained*, WIRED (July 2012), https://www.wired.com/2012/07/apple-v-samsung-explained/

Posner, Richard A. *Why There Are Too Many Patents in America*, THE ATLANTIC (July 2012), https://www.theatlantic.com/business/archive/2012/07/why-there-are-too-many-patents-in-america/259725/

History.com staff, *The Continental Congress*, (2010) HISTORY.COM, http://www.history.com/topics/american-revolution/the-continental-congress

Quinn, Gene, *An Old Patent Examiner Explains Poor Patent Quality*, IPWATCHDOG (Aug 2009), http://www.ipwatchdog.com/2009/04/17/an-old-patent-examiner-explains-poor-patent-quality/id=2651/

Lichtman, Doug and Lemley, Mark A., *Rethinking Patent Law's Presumption of Validity*, STANFORD LAW REVIEW (Aug 2007), https://www.researchgate.net/profile/Mark_Lemley/publication/228188392_Rethinking_Patent_Law's_Presumption_of_Validity/links/02e7e51eaa79346c23000000.pdf

Hise, Phaedra, *How the Wright Brothers Blew It*, FORBES (Nov 2003), https://www.forbes.com/2003/11/19/1119aviation.html

Price, Jr., William, *Reasons Behind the Revolutionary War*, Tar Heel Junior Historian Association, NC Museum of History (1992) taken from NCMEDIA, http://www.ncpedia.org/history/usrevolution/reasons

LIBRARY OF CONGRESS, *Wilbur and Orville Wright Papers at the Library of Congress*, 1901 to 1910, https://www.loc.gov/collections/wilbur-and-orville-wright-papers/articles-and-essays/the-wilbur-and-orville-wright-timeline-1846-to-1948/1901-to-1910/

Cornell Law School, https://www.law.cornell.edu/wex/intellectual_property_clause